# WARFIELD PRESS

PRESCOTT, ARIZONA

# COOKING ALINSKY'S GOOSE

## THE NEW CAPITALIST COOKBOOK

# CHARLY GULLETT

*For Amy...*

*"Do one of three things. One, go find a wailing wall and feel sorry for yourselves. Two, go psycho and start bombing... Three, learn a lesson. Go home, organize, build power and at the next convention, <u>you be the delegates...</u>"*

**Saul Alinsky** on the failure of the 1968 Chicago Democratic convention takeover...

# THE NEW CAPITALIST COOKBOOK

*Appendix*

*References*

# *Foreword*

I had the privilege and honor of speaking to about 3,000 of my fellow citizens on the April 15th TEA PARTY in Prescott, Arizona. To borrow a phrase, I urged everyone to express to the elected class that we are "...MAD AS HELL AND WE'RE NOT GONNA TAKE IT ANYMORE!" On the way to my truck, a man stopped me and asked "What exactly can I do, right now?" I did not at that time have a good organizational tool to recommend, but now with this book, I have that tool. Every person who has a dream of American freedom, financial independence and individual liberty, needs to read this book if for no other reason than the sake of their children and grand-children.

My friend Charly is a radical. A radical, not in the popular sense, but rather in the pure dictionary definition; relating to, or proceeding from a root or root cause, advocating extreme measures to retain or restore a political state of affairs. Charly is one of those guys who make you proud to be an American. As a radical, he is willing to use the Constitution, starting with the Bill of Rights, to organize other like-minded individuals and to join him in taking back the United States of America from a band of amoral Socialists.

Herein then lies a way to take the Socialist playbook and use it against them by leveraging what their principal activist/philosopher Saul Alinsky advocated. Charly is urging us to join him in the exercise of raw political power by combining both organized activism and the simple act of voter registration to turn the tables on Socialism. Much as Medusa seeing her reflection in Jason's shield was turned to stone, the tactics in this book can stop Socialism in its tracks. Not only is this book setting out a roadmap for conservative victory, it also empowers the great silent majority, to make our views, our virtues and our values predominant in the USA once again.

Incredibly, Charly has also discovered in a re-examination of Alinsky, that those of us who go to work every day, make our PTA's function, our churches sacred, and our businesses successful, are much better suited than anyone else to do the actual work of organizing a new American revolution. Many of us are justifiably outraged at what has happened recently in America, but let there be no anger without action. Organize first...organization leads to power and the exercise of that power leads to the defeat of our enemies. My favorite President, Ronald Wilson Reagan, had a very simple and straight-forward plan for the old Soviet Union, "We win. They lose!"

Like Reagan, we must face the enemies who are taking away our freedoms and destroying our sacred endowments. In facing this enemy we must state clearly and simply what is at stake and why we are right and more importantly, why they are wrong. We must express this at every opportunity and with absolute honesty and historical accuracy. Again and again we must demand that these founding truths be upheld and honored and defended, "... that all men are created equal, that they are endowed by their Creator with certain unalienable Rights, that among these are Life, Liberty and the pursuit of Happiness." And finally we must state clearly and unequivocally that we want no less than the destruction of our common enemies. Charly's plan, as laid out in this book is just as simple and straight-forward, and has the added benefit of using their own words, plans and tactics against the Socialist left to win this cultural conflict.

We must organize, re-invigorate our existing voters, register new voters, and get both old and new voters to the polls in 2010 and beyond. We must create the necessary political power, exercise that power and use it to recapture rational political thought in this country. Elections have consequences and it is clear we cannot survive the destructive consequences of Obama and his Socialist minions! You are holding in your hand the owner's manual for the peaceful revolution that can lead us back to freedom.

God bless the United States of America and God bless the patriots who will save her.

STARTING WITH YOU!

*Dr. Terry J. Lovell*
Prescott Arizona

# *Introduction*

The idea for the cookbook came to me as the result of a news story about Hillary Rodham (Clinton's) honor thesis at Wellesley College, (*"There Is Only The Fight...": An Analysis of the Alinsky Model* [1]*)*; its subject was long-time Chicago Socialist/activist Saul David Alinsky. The story broke information regarding the suppression of public access to the thesis for fear of Hillary Rodham (now married to President Bill Clinton) being associated too closely with Alinsky's radical left ideas. Wellesley College had dutifully complied with the request for suppression by changing the college's formal rules for thesis access. For many years the Rodham thesis was considered by many conservative pundits to be the 'Rosetta Stone' [2] of radical left politics.

In my own college days of the same period, I had read one of Alinsky's books and I remembered it as being somewhat radical; indeed, a little nutty. The book surprisingly is still in my library. It seemed completely logical to me at the time of the news story that Hillary Clinton, who probably started thinking about a presidential run even before her husband finished his first White House campaign, would want to distance herself from a radical like Alinsky in order to hold the broadest possible constituency of soft and hard Democrats.

A few years ago, as the thesis began to see the light of day, the news story, in my opinion, turned out to be a near miss. First of all, Rodham wrote the thesis the year she was transitioning from conservative Republican to conservative Democrat; the transformation into committed radical was not to be complete until her exposure in graduate school to more extreme activists and to Bill "I did not inhale..." Clinton.

The prolific British Fabian-Socialist George Bernard Shaw wrote that he cared deeply for the poor but you would not want to invite them to dinner as they would just as soon steal your spoons as look at you. [3] Similarly, Rodham did not at that time profess the 'love without limits' perspective for the plight of the poor. In fact, neither Rodham nor Alinsky had any faith in his radical program to change poor neighborhoods. She wrote hesitantly about her limited expectations for Alinsky's activist model for change...

> *"A People's Organization of local organizations*
> *can at best create new levels of harmony among*
> *its members and secure a few material gains. It*
> *is not oriented towards harmonizing competing*
> *metropolitan interests in a concert of*
> *government restructuring. Part of the reason*
> *why it is so ill-equipped is the lack of vision..."* [1]

Clearly at the end of his career and having failed at igniting anything remotely similar to class revolution, Alinsky was turning to the federal spigot for tax dollars and bureaucratic organization as a political surrogate for social change. Rodham made the following remarks in her conclusions on the direction of Alinsky's community radicalization...

> *Alinsky recognizes the impossibility of achieving*
> *social change at this time through the*
> *incremental means of power/conflict*
> *organizing. His supplementary plans call for*
> *federally-financed work projects on the order of*
> *the TVA."* [1]

This is hardly the stuff of revolutionary diatribe. Contrary to the news story, the Clinton's were avoiding any embarrassing association with young Rodham's borderline <u>*conservative*</u> musings that might be construed by the elite media as less than enamored with their lock-step Alinsky radical-chic. From the Clinton's perspective, it was better to be incorrectly assumed a radical leftist than correctly labeled any kind of conservative.

Within a couple of years after Rodham concluded her Wellesley thesis, Alinsky did return to his romance with revolution to write his opus magnum on radical activism *Rules for Radicals, A Pragmatic Primer for Realistic Radicals* [4]; but it was to reflect a much more radical strategy than the economically flawed TVA bureaucracy he suggested to a starry-eyed college girl.

Even knowing this, had the thesis been available and the story been reported accurately it would still have missed the point; the real news was that in spite of Rodham's doubts and Alinsky's initial failures, by the end of the Clinton Presidency the model had been used for four decades by Socialist Democrats who wiped the congressional floor with conservatives using many Alinsky tactics. It also seemed painfully obvious to me that President William Jefferson Clinton won two presidential races by cashing in Alinsky's political capital in social activism. More recently, President Barrack Hussein Obama demonstrated in 2008 he understood this model even better than Hillary Clinton. Consider some recent events... (*Alinsky excerpts are indicated in italic* [4]):

- Voter registration as revolutionary activism, first used in the 1940's by Alinsky's Industrial Areas Foundation (IAF) was affectively implemented by ACORN and others in the 2008 presidential election ("*Power comes from organization...*")

- Effective use of Karl Marx tactics to organize diverse groups; gays, lesbians, environmental wing nuts, pedophiles, abortion criminals, illegal immigrants, elite anti-American media, poor blacks, terminal welfare addicts, Islamic terrorists, Socialist apologists in academia, etc. (*"...seek out allies."*)

- President Obama's re-institution of the Reagan ban on carrying firearms in National Parks. President George W. Bush had reversed the ban just prior to leaving office. U.S. District Judge Colleen Kollar-Kotelly issued a temporary injunction, favoring a lawsuit brought by anti-rights gun-control and environmental activists. The premise for the injunction was the need for an environmental impact study by EPA (*"Make the enemy live up to their own book of rules..."*)

- Repeated *accusations* of war crimes, corruption, failure of conservative ethics, and ruthless corporate behavior, all championed by the mainstream media, without journalistic corroboration or professional editorial review (*"Keep the pressure up..."*)

- The reciprocal relationship of liberty (as enumerated in the Bill of Rights) and capitalism are no longer understood by the American public; indeed the words themselves have become anathema in both political and academic discourse while anti-American Socialist diatribe dominates the Democratic Party, mainstream media, and academia (*"Ridicule a man's most potent weapon..."*)

- Government bailouts, normally considered Socialistic, are used by a coercive Republican president and deemed 'essential' and appropriate policy (*"If you push a negative hard and deep enough it will break through into its counterside..."*)

- Lack of moral clarity has brought about a modern political madness where vicious foreign dictators like Venezuela's Hugo Chavez are perceived to be our friends and unapologetic domestic terrorists like Bill Ayers are given academic tenure while objective dissent by Governor Sarah Palin is viewed as dangerous and subversive (*"...identifying the enemy."*)

- Complete acceptance of 'anything goes' in San Francisco and other hotbeds of socialism, including the party-like costume and theatrical greasepaint atmosphere of gay anti-religious terrorists invading, insulting and disrupting church services (*"Stink up the place...A good tactic is one that your people enjoy..."*)

- The Republicans, sitting in the political cat-bird seat after 9-11, under constant pressure from the mainstream media and left wing hate blogs allowed Socialists to completely re-define the war on terror, American economics, and the immigration issue. (*"Pick the target, freeze it, personalize it and polarize it..."*)

In his conclusion to '*Rules for Radicals*' and writing of the perceived frustration of the middle class to resolve the dilemma of a lost generation, Alinsky could well be discussing problems of contemporary, rational, patriotic Americans struggling with the realities of a new Socialist millennia...

> *"They have seen values they held sacred sneered at and found themselves ridiculed as squares or relics of a dead world. The frenetic scene around them is so bewildering as to induce them to either drop out into a private world, the nonexistent past, sick with its own form of social schizophrenia—or to face it and move into action. If one wants to act, the dilemma is how and where; there is no 'when?' with time running out, the time is obviously now."*

At some point, it began to dawn on me one might be able to use the Alinsky model for change, but instead of targeting the destruction of capitalism, the target might be the downfall of socialism in America. Political tactics, like military tactics, are used by both sides regardless of the issue. On the eve of Alinsky's 100th birthday, it would seem fitting to reflect upon his obvious success with these tactics. Putting the Alinsky/Marx psychotic delusions for proletariat revolution aside, it seems to me if we really want to advance the notion of liberty, we could take a few pointers on strategic activism from the side of the battleground that is kicking our butts.

Besides...using Alinsky's own rules to achieve the defeat of socialism has a certain irony to it.

Here then are some suggestions for political change, seen through Alinsky's eyes, but with a view toward recapturing liberty in America...

# *Part I: Slice and Dice*

> *"...there are no rules for revolution any more than there are rules for love or rules for happiness, but there are rules for radicals who want to change their world; there are certain central concepts of action in human politics that operate regardless of the scene or the time...These rules make the difference between being a realistic radical and being a rhetorical one..."*
>
> -- Saul Alinsky, <u>Rules for Radicals</u> [4]

## *A Passion for Change*

The excerpt above was my first specific realization that in spite of the fact Alinsky was a radical Socialist; he was actually creating an activist model that had *nothing* to do with the political change he personally was seeking. Although he clearly intended for the book to foment Socialist change in America (and it eventually did), for the model to be successful, it was necessary for Alinsky to first divorce the process of activism from the thing to be activated, define and itemize that process, and then, in context, reconnect them to his agenda as though they were one. Everything in the book substantiated this. I believe, that once the model is again separated from his Socialist agenda, the rules are applicable to literally any political situation implemented by any political organization, even one in which the target for change is Alinsky's own Socialist America.

Consider this excerpt from a contemporary article by Ryan Lizza on Barrack Obama's training in the Alinsky method...

> *"(Alinsky's)...legacy is less ideological than methodological. Alinsky's contribution to community organizing was to create a set of rules, a clear-eyed and systemic approach that ordinary citizens can use to gain public power."* [5]

Activism is timeless and gold is where you find it. We should not reject the Alinsky strategies just because they have been used against us by the enemies of liberty. If we care about America and the inseparable relationship of individual liberty and capitalism, we need to embrace ANY realistic strategy or ethical tactic capable of success.

This is not advocacy for illegal action; nor was Alinsky's book. In spite of his embrace of ethical relativism ('...*in war, the end justifies almost any means.* [4]"), one of the things Alinsky was absolutely adamant about was the notion of working within the system...

> *"If the real radical finds that having long hair sets up psychological barriers to communication and organization, he cuts his hair..."* [4]

This was a revolution within a revolution in 1972. Although the roots of American Socialist-fascism go back to at least the time of Alinsky's childhood during the Woodrow Wilson administration, and are well-documented in the book *Liberal Fascism* [6], most of the 1960's radicalism was reborn with *The Port Huron Statement* [7] authored by the Students for a Democratic Society (SDS). In the sixties, Tom Hayden, Todd Gitlin, Bill Ayers, Bobby Seals, Bernadine Dohrn, John Kerry, Angela Davis and others used what are now considered traditional radical strategies (sit-ins, political rock concerts, the violence of 'non-violent' dissent, confrontation, domestic terrorism, and the de-facto anarchist strategy of civil disobedience); which frequently made the six o'clock news and harvested new recruits but, as Alinsky mused, created very little substantive change...

> "Spouting quotes from Mao, Castro, and Che Guevara...are as germane to our highly technological, computerized, cybernetic, nuclear-powered, mass media society as a stagecoach on a jet runway..." [4]

Alinsky realized traditional approaches "...create distance, promote frustration and lack cohesive organization [4]". Most of all, he realized the sixties activists failed to communicate with the people they were trying to activate. It was one thing to get a crowd of pot-smoking-hippie-anarcho-pacifists to execute a sit-in at a specific college in order to promote a student issue unique to that situation; it is an entirely different thing to organize and execute a bellwether change in national political policy. Alinsky proposed something else...

> "We will start with the system because there is no other place to start...A revolutionary organizer must shake up the prevailing patterns of...lives—agitate, create disenchantment and discontent with the current values, to produce, if not a passion for change, at least a passive, affirmative, non-challenging climate..." [4]

Alinsky's ethics were frequently enamored of Karl Marx philosophies; but his tactics were extracted from the type of revolutionary takeovers which successfully positioned socialism as world-wide political oppression. He literally leveraged power from historically documented revolutionary successes; to this he added some imagination and a bizarre and dark sense of humor (i.e. his book was dedicated to Lucifer whom Alinsky called the first successful radical).

Was Alinsky successful? Yes. Was he a Communist? Probably, but who cares? Changing the tide of socialism in America is not so much about Alinsky as it is about his methods of activism and how we might use them.

## *Reading the Rules*

For Alinsky activists, or anyone else, the inevitable pitfall is a lemming-like reading of the 'rules.' Alinsky lamented the pedantic use of both this and his earlier work, *Reveille for Radicals* [8], as a list of specifics for activism; they were not. His choice of the word 'rules,' used in both the title and text, is poorly conceived. 'Rules' are dogma by definition; at their worst, received uncritically and applied without free will. Free-will was one of Alinsky's key elements in activism.

Alinsky repeatedly prods the activist to use imagination *with the model* to first create conflict in your opponent, followed by more imagination used in response to the conflict. This is the foundation for his conflict/response model (actually an evolution in thought boosted from the Marx/Hegel dialectic model for thesis/anti-thesis/synthesis conflict). From experience, Alinsky knew a successful action in Chicago, applied uncritically, might easily fail in California; the difference between success and failure is how imagination is applied to this conflict/response model. In his chapter on 'The Education of an Organizer,' Alinsky laments the problem of training organizers and their failure to grasp this idea...

> *"There are no fixed chronological points or definite issues. The demands are always changing; the situation is fluid and ever-shifting...The problem with so many of them was and is their failure to understand that a statement of a specific situation is significant only in its relationship to and its illumination of a general concept. Instead they see the specific action as a terminal point. They find it difficult to grasp the fact that no situation ever repeats itself, that no tactic can be precisely the same."* [4]

Alinsky struggled with this issue for decades. Honing his training skills, his Industrial Areas Foundation (IAF) eventually developed a training program for organizers that stretched into a grueling fifteen month marathon. One of the biggest nuts to crack with new organizers was their lack of experience; young activists simply did not have enough experience with diverse groups to be dropped into new and unfamiliar neighborhoods and successfully organize a unique conflict/response model. The IAF training program was forced into creating artificial experience to supplant this void. According to Alinsky it frequently failed, but as these failures emerged, Alinsky took copious notes, and from the notes he synthesized an idea. He concluded there were qualities of organizers which were more useful than others, and while he might not be able to teach these qualities, identifying who had them was critical to who would be more likely to succeed than not. He knew that no organizer ever has a full grasp of all these virtues, but the good ones had a working familiarity with most if not all of them.

## Alinsky's Activist Virtues

- Curiosity
- Irreverence
- Imagination
- Sense of humor
- Vision
- Organizational (task management) personality
- Knowing the difference between strategy, tactics and negotiated results
- Perseverance
- Flexibility
- A serendipitous sense of adventure
- A sense of the meaning of life

Foregoing 'irreverence' for the moment, are these not the qualities of successful entrepreneurs? Indeed, are they not the qualities business managers, retailers and industrialists are constantly looking for in high achiever employees? Ironically, Alinsky's almost maniacal search for leaders to create a Socialist utopia was incredibly based on finding people with the very qualities which provided America with a successful foundation for liberty and capitalism. Even the notion of irreverence, while not taken literally by corporate managers, is often sought out as a virtue for perspective leaders. We just don't call it irreverence...we call it 'thinking outside the box.'

Although he did not use the phrase *empathic rapport*, it was a process that topped his list of qualities. He referred specifically to this experiential process in the life of an effective activist...

> *"Through his imagination he is constantly*
> *moving in on the happenings of others,*
> *identifying with them and extracting their*
> *happenings into his own mental digestive system*
> *and thereby accumulating more experience..."* [4]

Thankfully, the issues of imagination, rapport and experience in organizing and managing are far more familiar to hard-working Americans than to Socialist radicals. Business owners, entrepreneurs, designers, engineers and executives form the innovative and financial backbone of the American capitalist economy. From engineering to medicine, banking, manufacturing, marketing, science and industry, we routinely exercise these virtues of capitalism in our everyday lives because we value American liberty as the protector of capitalism and as the foundation of our success. There would be little in a fifteen month training program taught by Alinsky activists that would appear new to us; in fact, most of us would think they had plagiarized our own corporate training programs.

What is not so familiar to us is the idea of using our capitalist virtues and our imagination in conjunction with a model for overcoming the Socialist agenda in America. There are limitations to any plan and this one is no exception; in engineering we call this limitation *the error budget.*

What is perceived to be the objective opposition to socialism in America is not well-positioned to spend the enormous amounts of time necessary to organize the machinery of activism. We tend to parent our own children rather than use daycare. We start and run businesses. We learn how to use computer spreadsheets rather than play computer games. Rather than let property disintegrate into disrepair, we spend weekends doing our own maintenance on property that we own because we earned it and we are willing to spend the time to maintain and improve its value. Personal responsibility takes time. Make no mistake about this; a new movement of capitalist activism in America is going to compete for our weekends. But no matter how much weekend time we are willing to devote, we cannot succeed alone. As Alinsky repeatedly said, and it should become our mantra, *"...power comes from organization."* [4]

## *The War Against Liberty*

Don't expect recruiting to be easy. The whole idea of finding like-minded individuals has recently been stigmatized by the Department of Homeland Security (DHS) as 'extremist' (DHS Report, April, 2009). Secretary Janet Napolitano's hit job on conservative Americans is one more example of the loss of moral clarity where the real Islamic enemies of America are given favorable mood-lighting for a Kodak photo-op with the President while empowered Socialists in law enforcement shine a harsh light of interrogation on honest hard-working Americans. They consider us potentially violent even as President Obama publicly kowtows to the European cowards who have preceded him in Socialist complicity.

A lot of Americans realize this already, but just so it is not confusing to those who are new to this, Socialists here and abroad have declared social, political, financial, intellectual and military war on American liberty and capitalism.

What happened on 9-11 was the result of over a millennium of unprecedented psychotic mysticism based on totalitarian traditions. The attack on New York signaled Islamo-terrorist willingness to spill blood on American soil in order to perpetrate a tyrannical Islamic takeover in this country; this is their Jihad. It is not even obvious they need to spill much of their own blood in this effort. Consider the following...

> *"We have 50 million Muslims in Europe. There are signs that Allah will grant Islam victory in Europe – without swords, without guns, without conquest. The 50 million Muslims of Europe will turn it into a Muslim continent within a few decades."*
>
> Libyan leader Muammar al-Gaddafi
> Al-Jazeera TV, April 10, 2006

This process of Islamic world takeover by means of migration is no accident; in Islamic countries it is a specific strategy called *Al-Hijra*. With an Islamic birthrate of over eight compared to an American birthrate of less than two, is there any rational reason to believe the *Al-Hijra* now taking over European countries will be any different in the United States? Islam is already the fastest growing religion in the United States.

If you have not read it (and I suggest you do), the Islamic Koran is not just a religious work, it is a business plan for world domination. Their apologist American partners in this crime against humanity, Obama, Napolitano, Reed, Pelosi, Frank, Soros, the mainstream news media and all of their America-hating ilk have identified us as the enemy. We did not ask for this enemy status any more than we asked the government to enslave the next three generations of American taxpayers in unfunded debt, runaway inflation, financial fraud and intellectual bankruptcy. While they may not make the mistake of believing we will lie down for this, our ability to fend off this onslaught of Socialism is not a foregone conclusion.

Conservatives by definition do not like to see things change; this is at once our greatest strength and our most vulnerable characteristic. Our very nature is to be quiet, busy, and humble. When confronted by arrogant, emotional, noisy radicals, who often pass themselves off loudly as victims of one silly thing or another, we are usually so embarrassed by the situation we will often do whatever it takes just to quiet things down. The strategy is *intended* to put us on the defensive; to create a conflict and to elicit an expected response. This nonsense is pursued with threats and offers of negotiation until we concede the necessity to give something up, and then they back off...this is where we get victimized and consistently lose political and intellectual ground.

Conservatives are being manipulated into an untenable position of compromise specifically used to breathe life into this rationalization of inaction including apathy, loss of hope and a sense of powerlessness. The more we compromise, the more we back away from confrontation, *the more they get away with it.*

Over the last few decades as we watched the left organize, promote and actively participate in traditional street demonstration photo-ops, as well as the Alinsky activist litany of voter registration drives, proxy strong-arming, gonzo journalism, environmental fraud, and academic terrorism, it has been difficult for us to perceive their type of street theatre as productive in the ethical sense; and both ethics and productivity are very important to us. Ayn Rand identified the relationship of the virtue of productivity to individual liberty at least as early as 1961 in a presentation on Objectivist Ethics in America...

> *"...the three values which, together, are the*
> *means to and the realization of one's ultimate*
> *value, one's own life—are: Reason, Purpose,*
> *(and) Self-Esteem, with their three*
> *corresponding virtues: Rationality,*
> *Productiveness, (and) Pride."* [9]

Our failure to recognize the value of "purpose" in this political-activist context creates a loss of perspective in regard to directing the virtue of our productivity; this is something we risk at our own peril. As a result, the tentacles of President Obama's Socialist tax oppression and tyranny have been driven deeply into our daily lives and it is likely to get worse for our children; much worse. After four decades of out of control taxation fueled by inflation and government spending, we now have the three stooges running the White House and the Congress; Reed seems to think he has spent enough time cozying up to Code Pinkos to lead a military surrender; Speaker Nancy Pelosi is telling people illegal immigration is actually patriotic; and President Obama is sitting in the White House nationalizing the banking system, coercively taking over automotive corporations and spending money on pig stink faster than grease through a short goose.

I am going to use a term which will no doubt be regarded as controversial; the word is 'treason'. It is the greatest crime of which an elected politician may be guilty; to coercively legislate a confiscation of wealth in order to perpetuate the poverty of entitlement and the nationwide establishment of Socialism. This theft of American wealth is fueled by tax money directly, and indirectly through inflation, from those who worked for it, giving it to those who don't. Once Socialists get their hands on our money they use it on welfare programs for drunks, illegal immigrants, fools and drug addicts who proceed to spend the money to create bad art, more illegal immigrants, increased mortgage fraud for the unemployed clueless and for Socialist agendas in our public schools.

In my office, I have a sign that reads "Annoy a Liberal; Work, Succeed, Be Happy." I like it because it advocates a positive message for us while clearly defining the problem of socialism— specifically, the only thing socialism has ever given the world is welfare, failure, and misery. This has got to end. I say it's high time we do more than just get angry; we need to get active.

Are you fed up with this? I am.

## *Where Do We Go From Here?*

Instead of handing out condoms to grade school kids, we need to find a way to provide free firearms training to teachers to end the use of our schools as killing fields for every whack-job and unemployed wing-nut that decides he's misunderstood. Instead of giving out free abortion information to teen-agers, we need to be giving citizens in American/Mexican border-states free ammunition to defend themselves from the Mexican drug cartels, human trafficking criminals and violent Aztlán insurrectionists who are flooding across the border. Instead of oppressive taxation and printing-press inflation, we need to follow the Reagan model of supply-side economics, tax cuts and corporate incentives that pulled us out of the last recession caused by President Carter and his Kool-aid economics. We need to get active in order to make this and other necessary changes happen.

But you know what? All the Socialists, the illegal immigrants, the pan-handlers, the drug dealers, anti-American politicians and the winos are betting we are all going to go home after a hard day at work and do what? Nothing. And so far, they are correct.

They are hoping that we are beaten, that we don't really have the backbone our Founding Fathers showed England in 1775. You can see it in President Obama's face...right now he is showing more teeth than a flop-eared mule in a Prozac factory. They hope we are asleep at the wheel, sitting in front of the TV, cheering for O'Reilly, or Hannity, or Glen Beck, and doing absolutely...NOTHING.

So, I gotta ask you? What do you want to do? You want to do what they want? Or do you want to stand up and jam some real change down their statist, collectivist, and totalitarian Socialist throats?

Some of my suggestions for change are...

- National legislation similar to the Colorado Taxpayers Bill of Rights which not only puts limits on Congressional taxation but puts real limits on spending in the legislature. Hell, put *VISA* in charge of the Federal Reserve Banks and give them a credit card with a spending limit on it so that the next time they try to run up a trillion bucks in unfunded welfare spending the waiter shows up and says, "...I'm sooooo sorry, they won't accept this charge."

- Legislate protection for property owners and taxpayers so that *only* the 50% of American taxpayers who actually pay taxes may vote on what happens to those taxes and only property owners can vote on what happens to their property tax.

- Get the toleration for Socialist agendas and curriculum out of the National Board of Education, the US Department of Education and our schools by driving a national curriculum agenda based on liberty and Capitalism. We must begin to teach the understanding our economic role in liberty and our societal role in Capitalism, how the two are reciprocal partners in protecting individual freedom and how a free market can only be adequately taught at the expense of eliminating the intellectual crime and educational fraud that passes for free-thinking in our schools.

- Deny Socialists the three generations of tax slavery they have stolen from us and our children by organizing voter registration drives, electing rational candidates who will repeal the stimulus bill in 2010 and then kick the Socialist butthead out of the White House in 2012.

But, here's the problem…your list of changes…my list, who cares? We can waste a lot of time complaining about what is going on, how much the interest and the principal is going to cost the taxpayer over the next three decades, how wrong it is to pull out of the War on Terror, we can cry all day that the Federal Reserve Bank does not have the constitutional authority to bankrupt America with what it knows is inflationary assassination, and it will all be for naught, *because today the insane have the numbers to run the asylum.*

It was expected that the Democrats would turn out large numbers for the 2008 presidential election. What was not so expected was that over 10% of the Republican Party would vote for the loathsome little troll with the big ears and the Socialist track record in Chicago. What was worse, enormous numbers of conservative voters would either not register to vote at all, or having been registered simply did not vote. The ambivalence of those who sat out the 2008 election with their feet up at home instead of voting is the intellectual anesthetic socialism depends upon for success.

The Socialists will kill America with this unless we figure out how to get like-minded people to the polls to vote in the 2010 mid-term elections; the subject of the next section. Make no mistake about it; Alinsky's power through organization tactic is the most pressing element in taking back America from the brink of totalitarian Socialism. The key to this tactic is voter registration.

# Part II: New Recipes

*"...this sure doesn't look like Kansas, Toto."*
Dorothy, from the <u>Wizard of Oz</u>

## Power Comes from Organization

Any good organizational activity requires planning; revolutionary activism is no different. Three things need to happen in order for America to recapture liberty and capitalism; first, massive new voter registration; second, leverage both House and Senate wins in the 2010 mid-term elections by getting rational people to the polls; and third, author and execute on a new Contract with America that turns around the legislative insanity of the Obama administration. The big question then becomes, "...how do we do that?"

Alinsky tells us...

> *"Change comes from power, and power comes from organization. In order to act, people must get together...Power and organization are one..."* [4]

From Marx to Alinsky to Obama, the Socialists have networked diverse groups into focused organizations. Our task is no different; what separates them from us is the *focus on organization*. Individuality has always been the strength of both liberty and capitalism in America, and we have always revered competitive ideas, individual activities and unique process. At this juncture we no longer have the luxury of doing our own thing. We must now come together in order to save that which we hold dearest...the legacy of liberty and the morality of humanity for both ourselves and future generations of Americans. We must bring together our own *rational diversity*, the individual people and organizations that are liberty's last fighting chance for survival, and then *we need to have everybody on message*. From the Republican National Committee to local women's groups, from the National Rifle Association to community pulpits, from our work place to our soccer fields, the message is this:

## SOCIALISM is TREASON
## VOTE LIBERTY

Socialism is political terrorism; the stakes are the future of freedom, capitalism and enumerated liberty; win or lose, liberty or slavery, financial freedom or tax bondage, it has come to our generation to make the difference. Alinsky's message to us was political power is leveraged through organized constituencies; we need to get good people who have become discouraged, disenchanted, and disenfranchised off the couch and into the voting booth.

Want to do something important for liberty today?

Get your hands on a packet of Voter Registration forms and don't go anywhere without them. Get over your shyness about asking people if they are registered to vote. More than any other Alinsky tactic, ACORN and other community based activists groups dominated the last election by aggressively registering more pinheads than we registered patriots and then *they got them to the voting booth*. In most totalitarian countries power equates to violence; in what is left of an American democracy, political power is still a numbers game. We need a majority of people, and more importantly, we need a majority of *electoral states* to win elections. But are the votes really out there?

Even if we sacrifice our weekends and evenings to the cause of liberty, how do we know the numbers are there? Consider the following 2008 election statistics (sorry about the math, but bear with me for a moment, this is important and there is no test...)

- Total population in the US is approximately 303,824,640
- There are about 207,643,594 eligible voters in the U.S.
- There were 169 million registered voters for the 2008 Presidential election...
  86 million Democrat
  55 million Republican
  28 million others (independents, communists, green party, libertarians, etc.)
- About 124,000,000 actually voted in 2008 (about 73% of registered voters, 60% of eligible voters)
- 45,000,000 registered voters did not vote
- There are 38,000,000 eligible but unregistered voters
- Assuming the same 8/5/3 split of actual voters overlaid upon the number of registered no-show voters, there are probably 14,000,000 voters out there who would probably vote Republican if you could just get them to the polls
- Assuming the same 8/5/3 split of actual voters overlaid upon eligible but unregistered citizens, there are probably about 11,000,000 people out there who would probably vote a conservative ticket <u>if they were actually registered and we could get them to the voting booth!</u>

This means there are approximately 25,000,000 uncounted conservative voters in America, and when you consider only about *8,000,000 votes decided* the 2008 Presidential election, our strategy of voter registration should begin to fire your imagination. Even if this estimate is off by HALF, it is clear there are more than enough conservative voters out there to have reversed the election in 2008 if we could only have registered them and then made their presence known at the polls.

There are three nuts to crack in this situation; the 10% of Republicans who succumbed and voted for Obama's silver-tongued Socialism, the registered voters who did not get to the polls, and our like-minded citizens who are not registered. Each of these groups presents different challenges.

Inevitably, as we go about the task of finding and organizing these three groups of voters, we will be confronted by their excuse/rationalizations of why they don't register, don't vote, or vote badly. Be prepared; rationalizations are a trap Alinsky tried to avoid and we will need to do the same. We need to approach these groups with care. Again, Alinsky instructs us…

> *"It is primarily a subconscious feeling that the organizer is looking down on them, wondering why they did not have the intelligence, so to speak, and the insights, to realize that through organization and the securing of power they could have resolved many of the problems they've lived with for these many years—why did they have to wait for him?…but they are not real arguments, simply attempts to justify the fact that they have not moved or organized in the past…Rationalizations must be recognized as such so that the organizer does not get trapped in communication problems or in treating them as the real situations…Do not make the mistake of locking yourself up in conflict with them as though they were the issues or problems with which you are trying to engage the local people."* [4]

Let's look at what some of these excuse/rationalizations might be for each of our groups.

## *Obama Republicans*

- "I thought Sarah Palin was great, but I would die before I voted for a liberal like John McCain."
- "McCain didn't show any spine in the campaign and he really let Obama off the hook regarding Bill Ayers and Reverend Wright".
- "Bush lied, kids died. McCain was just a rerun of the Bush Administration."
- "I liked McCain, but Sarah Palin was a serious problem for me. Did you see the Katie Couric interview?"

- "It doesn't make any difference...they're all crooks. Screw 'em."
- "The Republican Party is no different from the Democratic Party any more, and Obama was campaigning for real change".
- "I saw Michele Obama on *The View* and I thought she was so nice and what great biceps."
- "Obama is an intellectual giant. He edited the Harvard Law Review. Oh my God!"
- "McCain is too old. He probably wouldn't live through the first term and Palin doesn't have the experience to take over. Did you see the Katie Couric interview?"

## *Couch Potatoes*

- "I had the flu..."
- "To do any good, you'd have to vote out every idiot in Washington and that ain't going to happen so why waste my time?"
- "My kids had the flu..."
- "I just could not get away from work..."
- "The Electoral College really elects presidents, my vote doesn't matter".
- "My car wouldn't start..."
- "It doesn't make any difference...they're all crooks. Screw 'em".
- "It didn't look like McCain could win anyway, so who cares?"
- "McCain is too old. He probably wouldn't live through the first term and Palin doesn't have the experience to take over. Did you see the Charlie Gibson interview?"

## Unregistered Conservatives

- "It's all a fraud.  Voting just encourages them".
- "The Electoral College really elects presidents, my vote doesn't matter".
- "I'm retired, it doesn't really affect me."]
- "I don't care..."
- "They don't care..."
- "It doesn't make any difference...they're all crooks. Screw 'em".
- "The Socialists are already in control, what difference does it make?"
- "It didn't look like McCain could win anyway, so who cares?"
- "McCain is too old. He probably wouldn't live through the first term and Palin doesn't have the experience to take over. Did you see the Katie Couric interview?"

These rationalizations fall into a few narrow categories; various forms of political apathy ("...my vote doesn't matter...", "...I don't care", "...it doesn't make any difference,"), lazy ("...my car wouldn't start...", "...I couldn't get away from work"), terminally stupid ("...Obama is an intellectual giant...", "...my kids had the flu"), politically deceived ("...they're all crooks", "...Bush lied, kids died", "...there is no difference between the two parties," etc.) and victims of media bias ("...Did you see the Katie Couric interview?").

## Terminally Stupid

Easy to identify, these rationalizations are plainly embarrassing even to the casual observer. These people are a waste of human flesh; you can try to bring them around but it is a dramatically misdirected use of your time.  Any high school teacher can tell you, it is impossible to save everybody; some people are lost causes, homeward bound for a wasted life; they might as well be Socialists. There is an old adage...ignorance can be fixed with a decent education; there is no fix for stupidity.  Do not debate people who, given the motivation to make something out of their lives, will instead take a nap.

## Lazy

The politically lazy, on the other hand, is not only easy to identify, but straight-forward in terms of how to get them on the program. If necessary, get them to fill out a voter registration form, take their name, address, (Email if they have it) and phone number and *commit to give them a ride to the polls*. More important than life...*follow through*. Appendix C has a Voter Contact Form in checkbox format. Using it will allow you keep track of the voter information and any re-contact you are able to use between now and the election. Take note of the location of their polling place (these are available from your local Elections Office, County Voter Registration Office, etc.), record their 'hot button' issues and offer suggestions to address those issues.

Interim re-contact can be very important. Political rallies such as the annual Patriots Day events, Tea Parties, or community service events sponsored by Rotary, VFW, women's groups can all be useful opportunities to bring folks back from the edge. Organize a voter fun day at the local shooting range, golf course or racket ball court. If you have space for it, organize a pot luck dinner. If you can afford it, rent a bus. At a minimum, be sure to call these folks back the week before the election, remind them who you are, arrange to pick them up and then ***deliver these voters to the polls on election day***!

## Political Apathy

This group is more complicated. Many otherwise productive, intelligent, contributing members of our community have simply given up on electoral participation. Their strategy is one of deliberate avoidance. Repeatedly bludgeoned by the punitive American education system, disturbed by high profile failures of trust in public officials, sometimes exhibiting the outward acerbity of failed romantics, and frequently the target of intellectual victimization of various kinds, the net result has driven these voters inside themselves. Your job is to get them out of there.

Although they may be registered, they often are not; so keep those voter registrations and voter contact forms handy. Those suffering from political apathy have already created well-worn circles in their life that insulates them from any experience forcing them to re-accept political reality. This cloistered and deliberate avoidance is specifically designed to prevent them from meeting you, so it is usually going to be a very short conversation with these people as they will reject you and the horse you rode in on very quickly. Be prepared for this; you will have a very small window in which to pitch participation. Build situational rapport first, hopefully based on some shared experience, or at least based upon the experience that has brought you together in the first place. Expand on this with a little cognitive dissonance (i.e. "...do you think its ok if Obama impoverishes you children for the sake of welfare recipients and illegal immigrants?") With the most recalcitrant apathy victims, the best you will be able to do is to obtain some contact information for use later. Take what you can, leverage everything you get.

For the more moderate forms of apathy, efforts at empathetic rapport will produce immediate opportunities for listening to what their hot buttons are all about and, once you open them up, they will have no shortage of them. Alinsky thought his ability to listen was his best suit. You should make it yours.

> *"I know that in a community, working as an organizer, I have unlimited patience in talking to and listening to the local residents. An organizer must have this patience."* [4]

Listening to their hot buttons is useful to engaging any of these groups but it is absolutely key with political apathy. In almost all cases, you will not only find yourself agreeing with their problems and issues; you will discover their hot buttons are actually yours. Years ago, my father gave me some really good advice. He said, "...you know, the best thing you have to give someone is yourself. It is OK to be you. As long as you are not putting on airs, people will relate to that and they will trust you. Everyone knows immediately if you are trying to be something you are not."

So don't fake it. Be up front when you have something to offer and LISTEN if you don't.

## *Media Bias Victims*

These rationalizations really break my heart. As citizens, we have great expectations that certain entities are to be trusted. The big ones are the government, the schools, our churches and our journalists. All have failed us in one way or another, journalists having done so in profoundly disturbing proportions. Our Founding Fathers viewed freedom of the press as one of the most important protections to enumerate in the U.S. Bill of Rights; so important the nuance of the freedom of the press is separated from freedom of speech...

> *"Congress shall make no law respecting an establishment of religion, or prohibiting the free exercise thereof; or abridging the freedom of speech, <u>or of the press</u>; or the right of the people peaceably to assemble, and to petition the Government for a redress of grievances."* [11]

And yet, this enumerated liberty, this critical right of the people, has been so severely compromised that the vast majority of the mean-stream media (in particular, public broadcast and cable media) is either completely in the tank for statist Socialism or is so wholly incompetent as to be of no value whatever. The 2008 election could have had no better example of this than the bushwhack interviews of Governor Sarah Palin conducted by journalistic frauds Katie Couric and Charlie Gibson. Similar hit jobs on a wide range of conservative subjects and candidates have been perpetrated by haters Bill Moyers, *The New York Times*, the hags on *The View,* almost anyone on NPR, the Huffington Post, MoveOn.Org and a long laundry list of others. Anyone who regularly gets their political information from these sources is likely to be a victim of media bias.

Media bias rationalizations can also be combined with other rationalizations, particularly political apathy. Listen carefully to it, let them get it off their chest, but don't get sucked into it. Do your jobs...be sure they are registered and they have a ride to their polling place on Election Day.

## *Politically Deceived*

Those that fall into the politically deceived category use complicated rationalizations combined with other rationalizations such as apathy or media bias victimization, but you can easily pick up on these as well. Frequently based on failure to perceive significant differences between the two political parties, this rationalization is attributed by them to a breakdown of American education combined with the mass media and Hollywood's incessantly cheerleading the Socialist agenda, pounding us with the notion of terminally corrupt politics. The rationalization ridiculously infers the Republican Party has joined the dark side *in collusion with the Socialists.*

In fact, both Fascism and Socialism are rival political criminals fighting a turf war in a fear-based society; they are not extensions of either liberal or conservative thought; they are the loss of both and the ascendancy of thug-based government. Fear-based, state-run regimes, either secular or mystical, always have the hallmark of government-forced individual sacrifice for the 'good of the country' (i.e. Mexico), or because 'Allah says it is so' (i.e. Iran). The so-called 'slide' of free society conservatism to the dark side is not through liberalism, it is through the failed economic policies of socialism exerted on the liberties of free market capitalism. Only when our capitalist economy fails through some enormous crisis manufactured by the Socialist agenda, can the nanny-state begin to leverage complete control over industry, business and education. They largely succeed in foisting this fallacy by controlling forums where no intellectual debate exists (news media and schools in particular, but also talk radio, magazines, etc.) and therefore they appear to have no dissenting opinion. Obama's mantra regarding the trillions of dollars of bailout money was "...this is a crisis only government can solve," is a fraud of unprecedented proportions even for the Socialists.

We are trapped in this one-sided dialog with a myopic and oppressive Socialist movement who operates on one of the oldest Marxist strategies available to activists. Comrade Lenin called it '*Advance Through Retreat,*" and as part of the Socialist playbook it has been used effectively against us for over 100 years. Marx invented it, Alinsky conceptualized it as a conflict/response model, and Obama rode it into the White House.

There is no question in my mind that many Republican leaders have for years allowed the party to move in the wrong direction rather than standing up for what their constituents believe; but the notion of collusion is a paranoid stretch and borders on conspiracy theory nonsense.

Let me just point out, the whole conspiracy thing is exactly what the Socialists want us to think. Their agenda is convincing us there is no longer a viable political process which offers choice in American politics and we must acquiesce to whatever the political sock puppets in Washington decide for us. Remember, Alinsky was willing to accept a "...*non-challenging climate*..." [4] This rationalization hands it to them on a silver platter. The more often it is used, the more often good people who feel disenfranchised by well-publicized political party failures, biased news, individual foibles and failures of elected officials, and the total disintegration of public school curricula, find that feigning aloofness to the electoral process allows them to distance themselves with a comfortable air of superiority *rather than admit they have been deceived*.

Here, as before, what will not work is to go down the path of any rationalization. The only place you can land with these arguments is to tell them their air of superiority sucks, they're stupid, they are an unwary partner to the Socialist agenda, they're lazy, or feigning aloofness does not change the fact they are cutting their nose off to spite their face; you are unlikely to win the hearts and minds of these folks with any of these comments. Stick to the plan; get out the registration forms, keep track of who you are talking to, *get them to the polls on time*.

## *Electing Good People*

Both voter registration and the logistics of getting people to the polls are clearly problematic but not insurmountable; the larger issue is finding viable candidates. Deep down (though they won't admit it) all the folks who suffer from these rationalizations know they have been had, and without explicitly stating that, addressing that issue is the key to turning them around. What all these people desperately need to believe in again is elected officials who hold dear the same values they do. In fact, we all need that. The question now becomes how do we get to there from here? It's easy to say we need good people to stand up and run for public office; it is somewhat harder to find them.

Let's go back to basics; these people are all around us, they participate in all the same activities we do…work, play, shop, worship, blog, community service. See Part IV for additional information on candidates and the vetting process.

## *Seek Out Allies*

Organizational recruiting by and for anti-American groups in order to find candidates and create voter blocs is not only an active and time-honored tradition on the left, it is on the rise and we are well behind the power curve on this issue. From New York City to San Francisco, Miami to Tucson, Shiite fundamentalists, Communist apologists, politicians and Socialist organizers are able to put a lot of people on the street, on the phones, in the blogs and most importantly, in the voting booths for several reasons. First and foremost, working American taxpayers are now supporting half the U.S. population who do not pay taxes; large numbers of unemployed people living off government taxpayer-funded welfare checks have a lot of discretionary time on their hands.

As noted earlier, we don't.

Something we do have, not available to Alinsky, is the extraordinary advantage of having the Internet as a communication vehicle. It is imperative that we use existing communication links for both business and personal life to provide a broad foundation for exchanging information. This must be expanded as much and as quickly as possible. You already know like-minded folks whom you have seen, talked to and emailed. You belong to Republican political groups, church groups, shooting ranges, veterans organizations, hobbyists, sporting organizations and health clubs to name a few. Look at your email lists and membership cards; Hell, look at your Christmas list. The American Solutions organization is currently offering website space for organizing tea-party like events in local communities; free blogs are available, and there are other venues of this type. The need for this mosaic recruiting network will not suffer procrastination without profound risk.

We need to find, communicate with and organize our fellow high achievers. As my good friend Dr. Terry Lovell often says, "...we must become evangelists for liberty." The success of our evangelism will be measured in voter registrations. Alinsky hit it on the head...

> "...a wide-based membership can only be built on many issues...In a multiple-issue organization, each person is saying to the other, "I can't get what I want alone and neither can you..." [4]

Once we register the necessary number of rational people, we must then get them to the polls. We must leverage our existing networks into poll participation. We cannot do this without you. Every rational American must make a commitment to locate, register and then deliver to the polls this lost sea of conservative voters. Use your imagination; use your feet.

# Part III: Shake and Bake

*"We will either find a way or make one..."*
—Hannibal

## *Radical Redo*

Let us assume for the moment our voter registration drive is proceeding as planned. Like Alinsky we must view this as one very important part of a larger mosaic of activism. If all we do is outnumber them at the polls next time, there are still substantial numbers of additional intellectual zeros and Socialists elites out there who can be activated by similar voter registration efforts. Their mean-street activism is what got us into this situation; without substantial change in the way it works, we will see a return of this again and again. Make no mistake about it; right now they know how to do this better than we do.

As I indicated in the introduction, Alinsky found noisy issues did get on the evening news; sit-ins, street demonstrations and more importantly, these events could effectively disrupt specific organizations, individual businesses and local neighborhoods. These disruptions not only win new recruits, but keep the individual targets too busy to launch counter-attacks. Long term, we must not only win elections, we must disrupt, and if possible, dismantle the systems of Socialism being used against us. This is a tall order. But again, Alinsky lays out for us the means by which we may achieve this end.  The meat of his organizational activism lies in a chapter called '*Tactics*'.

### Alinsky's First Rule of Power Tactics:
> *"Power is not only what you have but what the enemy thinks you have..."* [4]

This is essentially the old adage, the bark is worse than the bite. The bad guys have used this against us for decades.  Socialist organizers rely on disenfranchised social outcasts, failed intellectuals, psychological misfits, drug dealers, welfare addicts and winos to support many mean-street constituencies.  We are not going to be able to do that.   A lot of people recruited to the Socialist cause are quite frankly zeros.  Many of them are terminally unemployable and repeat offenders in the welfare office; we don't need them.  Many of them have nothing going in their lives in the first place, so when an organizer comes along and tells them they are oppressed victims of the wealthy, these isolated rejects suddenly find solace and identity in what appear to be like-minded travelers in their plight as victims.  Recruited into the fold, they develop a mission in life; they become part of the issue.

The mantle of issue-victimization is a great comfort to someone who has wasted their life.  Being able to act out frustration at their own failures and irresponsible decisions allows them to let off a little steam, and it feels good commiserating with their fellow derelicts.  One of the first obstacles the Socialist organizers of the Alinsky left had to overcome was turning the vulnerabilities of local plight into problem; social deviancy into political issue.  The radical activist uses these myriad forms of deviancy not only to recruit but to evolve new issues.

> *"...An issue is something you can do something about, but as long as you feel powerless and unable to do anything about it, all you have is a bad scene...Through action, persuasion, and communication the organizer makes it clear that organization will give them the power, the strength, the force to be able to do something about these*

*particular problems. It is then that a bad scene begins to break up into specific issues."* [4]

Misfits of society suffer from a chronic condition known as FUD (Fear, Uncertainty, and Doubt), and in a general sort of way...as individuals, they don't even like each other. By definition, social outcasts are mortally afraid of being identified, uncertain of their self-image within society, and seriously doubt they can overcome it by themselves. It is easy then for these weak links to fall into nanny-like organizations that provide a pseudo-nurturing environment for them. Only through this group hug are they able to hide their incompetence and become useful to the puppet masters of Socialism.

By exposing these incompetence's as individual flaws (the old 'Divide and Conquer' thing), each becomes less useful and less powerful to the organization.

### Alinsky's Second Rule of Power Tactics:
*"Never go outside the experience of your people."* [4]

As indicated earlier, experience is a key factor. Identify what experience both you and your people have or can easily obtain, examine the experience of others as models for your organization, then decide what you need to do, who can help you do it, and how soon you can get from here to there using what you have. Look around you for those who have organized corporate training, Lions Club community events, find professionals with accounting skills, legal backgrounds and marketing campaigns. Picking good people with lots of experience you can leverage is the best possible plan (see Part IV on Candidate Selection for more on this).

Alinsky's advocacy here is not intended so much as a teachable moment for appropriate radical action, rather it is an attempt at the avoidance of undesirable confusion, fear, and inevitable embarrassment of retreat. These are emotions I like in an enemy who has earned the disdain of cowardice, and our direction should be to drive the Socialist lemmings to distraction in this regard, which leads us into...

### Alinsky's Third Rule of Power Tactics:
> *"Whenever possible, go outside of the experience of the enemy."* [4]

By doing so, he suggested you fan the desirable flames of confusion, panic, terror, and hopefully, complete collapse. To Alinsky, the 'enemy' was always the status quo of wealthy, capitalist, corporate America, and by inference wealthy, white, Christian conservatives. Individual activism against the so called status quo manufacturing corporations almost by nature needed to be point-blank contact, typically identifying one central manufacturing location. Not so with retail corporations, nor with religious affiliations, both of whom have diverse points of contact. Our own strategy will need to identify appropriate contact points based on similar vulnerabilities (see Appendix A for a list of appropriate radical targets).

One thing Alinsky began to realize toward the end of his life was that there is a much larger and profoundly more insidious group of anti-Americans who are employed, have no more discretionary time than we do, and control a considerable amount of wealth. This group is the so-called 'liberal elite'.

Different from the rank and file of clueless Socialist Democrats, this elite are the principle irrational source of real political madness in this country and many exist within current power infrastructures; particularly academia, mean-stream media, legal/political professions, and of course Hollywood. There are always exceptions, but many of these lost souls are the result of childhoods which failed to bond with parental or stand-in care-givers at critical developmental points, and having grown into dysfunctional adults—psychotically look to government as a surrogate nanny-state. Dr. Lyle Rossiter, Jr. has thoroughly detailed this analysis in his book, *The Liberal Mind* [10] which reveals "...the madness of the modern social crime for what it is: a massive transference neurosis acted out in the world's political arenas, with devastating effects on the institutions of liberty." If you have ever heard yourself saying, "...how can these idiots possibly vote for Obama?" then I highly recommend Rossiter's well-documented work on this clinical examination of political lunacy. One reading of Rossiter's book held up to Obama's childhood tells you the whole story.

More broadly, are legions of left-wing, radical Socialist organizations in America. Many of them are without surprise located in New York City, San Francisco, Los Angles, Tucson, and Seattle. A growing number of radio and television stations, internet website blogs, businesses and churches are breathing fire into hate speech which supports both materially and intellectually anti-American themes in general and Socialism, Islamo-terrorism and illegal immigration in particular (again, a partial list of some of these organizations is included in Appendix A).

Our actions must target all these groups, businesses, clergy, and internet for actionable events with disruption as the result. This is the last thing they expect to happen; to be targeted and publicly exposed as the clueless, small-minded, anti-American hate groups they actually are.

### Alinsky's Fourth Rule of Power Tactics:
*"Make the enemy live up to their own book of rules."* [4]

This is one of the most powerful political tactics Alinsky stumbled upon. Virtually everything and every organization adhere to some kind of rule book. Corporations have everything from business plans to articles of incorporation, local clubs have mission statements, even the loosest group of wing nut Socialists have the Marx manifesto or something equally irrational. Even La Network Campesina with a half-dozen radio stations throughout the southwest has a bottom line and a marketing plan with consumers and a board of directors to whom they answer.

Examination of their rule books provides the action plan agenda. Non-profits and religious organizations are vulnerable to their mission statements and their profitability; churches and mosques also have very specific rule books like the Bible and the Koran which provide challenging goals for all their fallen doves; corporations are vulnerable to their board of directors, their expense reports, markets and consumers; and everyone from local radical groups to the Democratic Party is vulnerable to lobbyist legislation. The EPA has fingers in a lot of things they have no business in touching, and someday we will want to cut them off; but in the mean time, we need to thump all these Socialist morons on their little pinheads with their own little rule book. You can find public policies on the corporate website, lists of their board directors, and they often advertise their best clients (who can be used for serious leverage). The federal government has all its rule books online. Start reading.

### Alinsky's Fifth Rule of Power Tactics:
*"Ridicule a man's most potent weapon."* [4]

Nobody likes to be the butt of a joke, much less ridiculed, which in our context, is the political form of laughter on intellectual steroids. Remember that Alinsky's main strategy was the imaginative use of the conflict/response model. Ridicule is a very powerful form of conflict initiation and typically can always produce a response of some kind; properly applied it can produce exactly the response you are looking for in a given situation. Obama prides himself on being a great orator; he is in fact little more than a hack propagandist for Socialism. Imagine his reaction if the public starts viewing him as a third-rate high school debater? When this happens, suddenly his jokes are not that funny, his ideas are thread-bare, his ideology is seriously suspect, his policies become frightening and his wife's biceps become threatening.

Alinsky found that once you have the target dancing to the desired response, it then can be further leveraged to force negotiation or to create new conflict. If your goal was to negotiate something (be sure you have that list prepared ahead of time), get what you want, you're done, go home early and plan another event. If you just want to keep them busy, then keep applying new and ever more creative forms of conflict-based ridicule and response until they self-destruct.

***Alinsky's Sixth Rule of Power Tactics:***
   *"A good tactic is one that your people enjoy."* [4]

In a general sort of way, we are going to enjoy all of this, even the hard work, because *we're doing the right thing.* Consider the following story from our own history.

> *In the early morning hours of Sunday April 19, 1775, Ralph Waldo Emerson's grandfather, the Rev. William Emerson was wakened from a sound sleep by a rider on horseback. Dr. Samuel Prescott was calling to him that the British regulars were on the march to Concord. After years of tax oppression, their intent was to force colonists into submission; the first step in this type of tyranny was to be a confiscation of all Massachusetts firearms. Having already sworn allegiance as a Minuteman to the local Committee of Safety, the Rev. Emerson dressed, then purposefully picked up his rifle and solemnly joined other Minutemen from Concord on the old North Bridge to face what would become the most far reaching military engagement in the history of freedom. As rumors swirled about and courses of action were discussed, Rev. Emerson yelled, "Let us stand our ground; if we die, let us die here." Standing ground in this case, meant they would stand up to what was at the time the largest, most powerful army in the world. Encouraging a frightened 18 year old Harry Gould, the Reverend said, "Stand your ground Harry! Your cause is just and God will bless you."*
> Patriots Day, 4.19.2009, Prescott AZ

As Americans, we love this kind of thing, because to us it is the essence of what America is all about; average people just like us, standing up against tyranny. We are motivated by this kind of thing and our actions need to reflect and be based on these roots of liberty. The Socialists are always about victimization and all the negative connotations associated with their psychotic irrationality. We are about the success of winning liberty for all people using the most positive elixir in the history of the world, the U.S. Constitution and its Bill of Rights. Putting our boots on the necks of criminal despots and their organizational minions should be fun.

What you want to avoid is anything that can get you into legal trouble. Our intent is not to break the law so much as it is to break the back of socialism in America. We can't do that from jail. Do not depend, as the left has done in San Francisco, on having an elected mayor who is going to give you a free ride on minor legal infractions; if anything, we can depend on the idea that the only free ride we will get is in the squad car if we are not real careful. So consider things within the context of law that are both fun and outrageous.

Years ago, Prescott author and firearms activist Jon Haupt wrote a wonderful piece called *5 Minutes to Freedom!* It is a very short and very sweet activist cookbook for the Second Amendment folks. Like Alinsky, Haupt's strategies can be applied to any political activist situation. It is well worth reading and is provided in Appendix B. Read it, it will change the way you look at activism.

A good example is throwing whip cream pies at the idiots when they are speaking at public events (note: locating a local media person who is with you, or at a minimum can keep their mouth shut ahead of time, and then getting them to the event for the pie throwing will help immensely). "Booing" is absolutely a protected form of freedom of speech; use it aggressively. Alinsky took great pride at one point in threatening to have a "fart-in" at a public event (see his book to truly appreciate the use of this liberating tactic). Organize a 'free subscription action' and deluge an organization with free subscriptions you have signed them up for using your existing magazines, or use the magazines in the doctor's office, your mechanics waiting room, or any junk mail you get at home. Have a good time, but get on with it.

***Alinsky's Seventh Rule of Power Tactics:***
> *"A tactic that drags on too long becomes a drag."* [4]

Try not to have too many meetings; endless meetings tend to drag the entire event into what is known as 'paralysis of analysis'. My own experience has been that exactly three meetings allow enough organization to be successful; pick the best people you can, and then use the first meeting to assign tasks. Just before the event hold the second meeting to see if the tasks are complete and to see if any diving catches are required at the last minute. Execute on the event and then hold the third post-action meeting as a debriefing to examine how the event came off and to pass some beers around (either for celebration of success or to console your troops for disaster).

Also, as mentioned before, have specific goals for your actions clearly in mind, write them down, be ready to negotiate them when you feel the time is ripe. Strike hard, strike fast, don't get bogged down. Getting hung up in a long term action will only prevent you from going after new opportunities. Fundamentally we are out of time already. Use what we have wisely.

***Alinsky's Eighth Rule of Power Tactics:***
> *"Keep the pressure up."* [4]

This is self-defining and goes with any action we take (excepting Rule Seven). Intensity is a key element to any action. If necessary, create waves of volunteers instead of having everybody on the street at the same time. The media, even one complicit in Socialism, can be your best friend here; they are bloodhounds for the front page and the lead story. Good continuous action, well targeted and intensely executed is something the media cannot resist. The smaller your town, the more likely your action will be the most interesting thing happening today.

Again, the conflict/response model is in play here in a continuum. The more responses there are to your action, the more conflict exists, followed by additional responses, etc., etc., etc. To remodel the classic McLuhan message; *the process is the pressure.*

**Alinsky's Ninth Rule of Power Tactics:**
> *"The threat is usually more terrifying than the thing itself."* [4]

Years ago I worked at a small Arizona college that was fortunate to have an excellent Gunsmithing School. Part of the program was to hold an annual gun show in the school's athletic gymnasium and was intended to provide the students with the opportunity to organize local commercial events, gain some experience in point of contact sales and develop good business skills. This particular show occurred during the second Clinton campaign, and the wife of the man who was the head of the local Democratic Party organization made exactly one phone call to a college official and threatened to make the gun show an agenda item in the upcoming campaign unless the show was cancelled.

My sense is the gun show (which the college had sponsored for decades) could not by itself have been so big a campaign issue that the local area would have suddenly become the Socialist hotbed of Arizona because of it, but the college did cancel the show. At the time, the college was canvassing the county for a bond proposal to expand academic services and they were working both sides of the street to make that successful. Sacrificing the gun show seemed a minor inconvenience compared to the $60 million dollars in the bond. The threat worked, the gun show was shut down, the college got its bond, and the threat did the trick without the anti-gun idiots lifting one more finger than it took to make the one and only phone call that went to the college.

What's the old saying from the sixties? "Follow the money." Pay attention to what is going on in your community; in particular know to whom and where money is moving. Leverage information to your advantage. Make some phone calls.

**Alinsky's Tenth Rule of Power Tactics:**
> *"The major premise for tactics is the development of operations that will maintain a constant pressure upon the opposition."* [4]

Although not dramatically different in tone from Rule Eight, Alinsky here was trying to justify the need for tactics by defining the premise, but then fails to provide a premise. He infers that somehow the development of operations is the premise, but does not elaborate on it. He does say, "... It is this unceasing pressure that results in the reactions from the opposition that are essential for the success of the campaign...action is itself the consequence of reaction." The tactic buried here is the process of pressure being applied to the target in order to elicit a reaction (stated and discussed elsewhere), but it can be supposed that 'development of operations' could be construed to be taking notes as you go on what works and what does not. Notes are good; mental notes are better.

### Alinsky's Eleventh Rule of Power Tactics:
*"If you push a negative hard and deep enough it will break through into its counterside(sp).* [4]*"*

This is a goofy way of saying this, but then, Alinsky had his goofy side. What he was trying to get at here was an expansion on the idea of creating enough intense conflict in your target that it causes reactions so perverted that the target almost literally shoots itself in the foot. Alinsky's example in the book was a corporation that he got so jived up they burglarized his home and the IAF with a group so inept the police were able to immediately determine who was involved (including Alinsky's targeted corporation).

The way Alinsky tells it, they did not press charges, but elected instead to leverage Rule Nine (...the threat is worse than the thing itself) to threaten the corporation with exposure of the crime followed by congressional review if they did not agree to terms. Unwanted public exposure is a powerful tactic that can bring the great to their knees.

This is a tough one to plan on, and tougher to actually plan. To read Alinsky one gets the impression this is a slam dunk; it is anything but that, although along with properly applied imagination, it can happen at fortuitous moments. In the end it is really only one measure of how successful your action is at a given point. However,

"...stupid is as stupid does"; be prepared to leverage whatever you get. Imagination, imagination, imagination...

### Alinsky's Twelfth Rule of Power Tactics:
*"The price of a successful attack is a constructive alternative."* [4]

This is like the target strangling you with your own action. The whole idea of the conflict/response model was to put pressure on the target in order to illicit an unprepared response; THEIR UNPREPARED RESPONSE, not yours. You want them to look bad and continue to look bad for as long a time as possible. Remember that the target wants you to go away and leave them alone so they can go right back to doing whatever quacks their ducky. To force you into providing a quick acceptance speech is to create a situation where you go away and they have plausible deniability because it is you who is providing the endgame response to the conflict, not them.

Without the continuum of the conflict/response model bouncing back and forth between you and the target, there is very little to be gained either in the media or in the decision room. Don't take yes for an answer.

### Alinsky's Thirteenth Rule of Power Tactics:
*"Pick the target, freeze it, personalize it, and polarize it."* [4]

Arguably, this is Alinsky's most famous statement; deservedly so, it packs great power. Essentially Alinsky was, in his verbose manner, first trying to say any group does a substantial amount of buck passing when it comes to authority to do things and this is doubly true when you introduce the stress-related actions of conflict/response. One of the best leaders I ever worked for was an Intel Corp. manager named Lionel Smith. Bumping up against a problem that required me to pull a decision out of a large organization, Lionel told me, "...be prepared, there are a hell of a lot of people who can say no; there is probably only one who can say yes. Your job is get him on the phone."

Actionable targets are no different from the guy I had to get on the phone. There are multiple layers of blame in government and politics; identifying a specific target in the network of misdirection is critical to the success of the action.

'Freeze it...' means your action must focus on specific blame to the exclusion of all others who are to blame as well. Freezing the target is to isolate it and force both them and the issue into the public eye. Don't' get mired knee-deep in too many targets; it will drain your resources and fail to produce results. Rest assured, the other blame holders will show up soon enough in support of their collective crime and your target. Stay focused, drive it deep.

Personalizing the target puts a face on the issue. We all rail against the huge monster of Socialism and set our hair on fire about the mortgage crisis, but somehow when you paste Obama's picture, or Chris Dodd's picture, or Barney Frank (egad!) on an issue, it suddenly becomes much more fattening. Barney Frank managed to help create an economic crisis that among other things resulted in General Motors selling off its corporate jets and requiring executives to fly tourist class. It would seem like justice if congress were required to do the same. I'd like to see Barney Frank try to park his prodigious and well-used dairy-aire into steerage.

Personalizing an action also makes it much easier to polarize the issue; the two go hand in hand. My good friend John De La Cruz who spent many years in the used car business told me that when you are selling a used car, you approach the sale as though "...it is made out of solid gold" but when you are buying a used car "...it is made out of chopped liver". Every item on your action list needs to position the target in the worst possible light. For Alinsky and his irrational ilk, this was a substantive challenge, as they were (and are) constantly targeting for destruction the good of America; we are not, our Socialist target is evil and that makes our job easier.

Here in Prescott, Arizona we have a small but vocal and visible group of idiots who dress up in black and stand on the sidewalk in front of the county courthouse on Fridays. They carry anti-war, anti-American placards. Let's assume I had picked them to publicize their idiotic position of surrender in the War On Terror (oops, pardon me, I meant to say Foreign Man Caused Disasters). I don't know if they even have an official group name (but I would find out). However, complaining to anyone in general about the 'women in black' neither personalizes nor polarizes the issue. I would need to find a name, and I would need to personalize the target (that one person) by finding a way to demonize him/her relative to the issue I had chosen.

In war, it's all about angels and demons.

# Part IV: Picking Ingredients Wisely

**Mongol General**: *"...Conan! What is best in life?"*

**Conan**: *"To crush your enemies, see them driven before you, and to hear the lamentation of their women."*

I am not big on re-inventing the wheel; particularly when time is of the essence. It is far more efficient and will typically get you to the same place using what is right in front of you. I think we have everything we need to do this. In the end, it will depend not on the availability of the (Alinsky) tools, but on our willingness to use them. For many of us, this is new territory.

The greatest opportunities for political success and at the same time our greatest vulnerabilities in this effort are our public officials, both candidate and incumbent. Any vetting process can and should utilize specific questions based on current issues intended to produce candidates with values (and hopefully track records) to match our agenda of defeating Socialism. Based on past failures, my feeling is...current question and answer vetting agendas are not up to the task. I think we need a new list of vetting questions. As indicated earlier, Alinsky struggled with selecting the right people with the right attributes and picking candidates is just as difficult.

Even if we go out, find and register enough voters to overcome the Socialists, even if we locate candidates we believe would make good choices based on American values of decency, how do we know they will follow through once they get elected and arrive at our local city councils, state legislatures, and that cesspool they call Washington DC?

The short answer is we don't know; never did, never will. OK, there are no guarantees, so what? I think we already know what is going on now is really bad. How much worse will this look if we do nothing?

So let's look at what tools are already in our midst to help us get from here to there. I think the vetting process could use a big dose of something called *"The Liberty Poll"* authored by publisher and author Alan Korwin, attorney Michael P. Anthony, and columnist Vin Suprynowicz (see Appendix D). These questions are straight from the hip and not the kind of anemic snake pap that passes for investigative journalism these days. A few examples...

> *Q. Would you support criminal penalties?*
> *a) for politicians who violate their oath of office;*
> *b) for bureaucrats who act outside the powers delegated to them?*

> *Q. Should someone who has sworn an oath to preserve, protect and defend the Constitution, but who then votes to allocate tax funds to programs or departments not authorized by that Constitution, be removed from office?*

Tough questions for tough times; The Liberty Poll can be used as is for the specific issues it addresses, but by example can also be used to formulate other issue-based questions. By vetting our candidates in this manner, at least we get candidates who appear to be on the program for liberty and justice for all.

From the beginning candidate selection has been a crap shoot, we all know that. Sometimes we got lucky, most of the time we did not. We have had Tammany Halls, local corrupt caucuses, candidacy vetting, smoke filled rooms, community organizers, and cocktail parties, whore house conventions, back room promises and "Change We Can Believe In." In the end, the candidates did just what they pleased. No culpability, no responsibility, very little exercise of constitutional recall and precious little redress.

A few examples of what pleased Obama before and after the election:

- His absolute promise to NOT raise taxes on anyone who earned under $250,000 a year, then raising taxes on tobacco affecting the lowest quintile wage earners in America. He has now made other aspersions to lowering that number as necessary
- His pledge to accept only public campaign financing then accepting private financing anyway
- His pledge not to use corporate lobbyists in his administration, then issuing waivers for the lobbyists he "needed"
- His pledge to eliminate legislative earmarks and then signed a stimulus with $5.5 billion dollars buried in 9000 earmarks which no elected official in congress read prior to the vote
- His campaign pledge to save jobs and then his 2009 presidential advocacy of the Waxman-Markey Cap and Trade bill which will kill jobs across all American industry and businesses

Obama is a political sociopath; no lie is too big to compound, and no American ideal is too great to destroy. There is no morality in this individual and no remorse in his agenda for the financial destruction of American wealth.

Once there was hope; In 1994 Newt Gingrich led a political charge called *"The Contract with America."* For those of you who do not remember this, during the first Clinton administration, congressional incumbents and many candidates agreed to execute on a specific political agenda in the first 100 days after taking office…IF voters would put them there. The contract had some great stuff in it; congressional reform, education, crime, etc. The agreement was, "…if we don't follow through, boot us out". Voters did their job; an enormous and historic number of Republicans were either elected or re-elected, and Newt and the gang followed through by introducing the bills in the contract. Not all the bills passed, but it was an interesting first time contractual dialog with Washington D.C. and the voting public.

*The Contract with America* was historically unprecedented in any government. As Speaker of the House, Gingrich told the Democrats they could count on Republicans to cooperate when there was agreement (specifically when the Democrats agreed with Republicans) but there would be no Republican compromise on issues where the two parties disagreed. At the time, it was the most significant line in the sand ever drawn in Washington DC.

Alinsky would have looked at that and said, "…we can kill them with this rule book." Lines in the sand are rule books in the making; and good rules are good ideas when you have people with enough spine to follow through. One of the early victims of Alinsky's rule book strategy was Newt Gingrich who resigned for failing to live up to a rule book about marriage which President Clinton refused to read.

While the *Contract with America* was a profoundly innovative and imminently constructive approach to changing politics as usual, somehow America still arrived in 2008, where a Republican President had spent eight years advocating amnesty for illegal immigrants in order to pick up votes, compromised the Bill of Rights by saying he would sign a new assault weapons ban if Congress would only send him the legislation, and before leaving office danced the Socialist bailout boogie with the Republicans in congress and Obama supporting him, including "The Great Compromiser" Senator John McCain. It was Marxist business as usual; vote buying, implementation of Socialist tax agendas, rampant economic oppression by professional politicians; pure Bolshevik.

We have reached not just a moment of great change, but a precipice of no return. It took the entire length and agony of human history just to get the world to a small bridge in Concord Massachusetts where people like us...businessmen, farmers, laborers and clergy stood up and said the oppression stops here.

I believe a new kind of *Contract with America* is in order, but this time with some serious teeth in it for those who stray from the path of liberty. The contract needs to reflect several very important things; first, it must be broad enough to effectively repeal Obama's existing Socialist mandates and legislation, and short enough and in plain English so even a politician can understand it. Second, it must have the necessary teeth to put the fear of God into politicians if they deviate from the contract; specifically financial repercussions and, if possible, mandatory jail time. Consider what this contract might look like...

### *EXAMPLE CANDIDATE CONTRACT*

*1.        On the first day of holding office, I will introduce and/or support a bill legalizing all aspects of this contract and requiring congressional office holders to include this contract in both US House of Representative and US Senate Ethics rules.*
*2.        On the second day of office I will introduce and/or support a bill to repeal criminal tax legislation for bailouts or stimulus packages passed during the Obama or Bush administration.*
*3.        On the third day of office I will introduce and/or support a bill requiring all parties who received money from stimulus packages or bailouts to immediately pay this money back. In the case of businesses, banks or others who have subsequently gone out of business, the executives who accepted those tax monies but did not pay them back, will be brought before debtors courts and their assets will be liquidated and their assets returned to the Congress. This will include asset forfeiture for offshore assets as well as spousal assets.*
*4.        On the fourth day of office I will introduce and/or support a bill criminalizing political collusion of elected officials and their staff who were culpable in congressional committees for allowing and encouraging the banking and mortgage/housing industry to make loans which precipitated*

the economic crisis of 2008 and beyond. Penalties for this collusion will be the same penalties specified for violation of this contract.

5.	On the fifth day of office I will introduce and/or support a bill requiring banking and all other lending institutions to lend no more than two dollars for every one dollar they hold in assets.

6.	On the sixth day of office I will introduce and/or support a bill which outlaws the Federal Government "pork" and "earmarks" for state or local programs/projects not tied directly to national infrastructure or security.  This bill will contain the same punishments in this contact criminalizing each elected official who perpetrates such legislation.

7.	On the seventh day of office I will introduce and/or support a Taxpayers Bill of Rights to permanently limit new legislated taxes to an amount equal to or less than 5% of the previous years tax revenues and limits congressional spending (excepting military emergency or national health emergency) to a non-deficit increased balanced budget.

8.	On the eighth day of office I will introduce and/or support a bill to require popular (not representative) votes on all new Federal tax proposals exceeding an impact to the taxpayer of more than 1% of the GDP and specifically prevent those who do not pay taxes from voting on any such proposed tax legislation.

9.	On the ninth day of office I will introduce and/or support a bill to permanently abolish the Federal Department of Welfare.  Any revenue remaining after dissolution of that department will be evenly distributed to American History teacher salaries throughout the country.

10.	On the tenth day of office I will introduce and/or support a bill which permanently repeals and dismantles the National Firearms Act and prohibits any Federal congressional elected politician, Federal legislative body or Federal court from introducing legislation or hearing standing on prohibition, restriction or possession of any type of firearm or ammunition by non-felon Americans.

**On penalty of my failure to execute this contract, I agree to:**

•	IMMEDIATELY resign from public office

•	ACCEPT lifetime banishment from holding public office again

•	VOLUNTARILY accept incarceration at hard labor in Federal Prison for a period of not less than ten years

•	VOLUNTARILY agree to pay (or spend the rest of my life trying to pay) a fine of ten million dollars (in 2008 dollars) per instance of my abuse and neglect of this contract. Please initial your understanding of each item and then date and sign below. Thank you very much. Now get to work.

*  *  *

Of course, most people would read that and have a good laugh; no politician worth his graft and payola would sign this; and isn't that the problem? The trick, as usual, is to get a Washington politician or even local political hacks to get behind anything (let alone sign something) that resembles a pledge for responsible behavior. Although it seems odd doesn't it that we have achieved a moral and political conundrum where the right thing to do is selectively ignored and the wrong thing becomes radical chic?

These days it is a fairly tough proposition just to get Republicans to act responsibly when they open their yaps about another Republican. Ronald Reagan's golden rule used to be that "...no Republican should speak poorly of another Republican." Too bad John McCain and his people didn't adhere to this simple rule. What they have done to Sarah Palin, in my opinion, is far more ruthless and despicable than anything Couric or the rest of those media morons could have dreamed up. At least you can depend on the Socialists to actually be Socialists and you know enough to hide the hard cash when they are in your home. It is an entirely different thing for conservatives to turn on each other like political piranhas in a feeding frenzy. The Republicans never seem to get this.

Note that what has transpired with Governor Palin is right out of Alinsky's *Rules for Radicals*. To date she has been challenged by over twenty ethics charges, many of which were thrown out as ridiculous. Five of the continuing saga of filings have been charged by the same person who has clearly figured out how the process works, understands both the emotional and financial impact to Governor Palin, the State of Alaska and the Republican Party. Palin announced this last month that the one-half million dollars in attorney fees has decimated her family and has served to provide a psychotic left-wing media with regular headlines. In Alinsky terms, the Alaska Ethics manual was the rulebook, the target was identified as Palin, the issue was frozen (each time a different ethic complaint was filed), Palin was personalized as the only responsible party, and the media has dutifully polarized the issue.

The entire premise of this book is that we do the same thing back at them, using exactly the same tactics, achieving the same well-proven results. Imagine the stink if Speaker Nancy Pelosi was suddenly faced with 10,000 ethics charge violations? Impossible? Not really. Consider that one motivated person with a home computer in Alaska created 25% of all the time, millions of dollars of money and effort to answer Governor Palin's ethics charges. If the Democratic Party isn't considering buying this cretin another computer, they are dumber than I think they are.

More importantly, what are we doing? Why aren't we locating the ethics violation rulebook on the websites in our home states and the federal government and filing charges against all the idiots that have tanked the economy, taxed our children, and titillated the welfare addicts into voting a totalitarian endgame into the White House?

Want to join us in a little political ethics management? Here is the website for the Senate Ethics Manual…

http://ethics.senate.gov/downloads/pdffiles/manual.pdf

Here are the current members of the Senate Ethics Committee (111th Congress)…

**DEMOCRATS:**
Barbara Boxer (Calif.), **Chairman**
Mark Pryor (Ark.)
Sherrod Brown (Ohio)

**REPUBLICANS:**
Johnny Isakson (Ga.) Ranking Member
Pat Roberts (Kan.)
Jim Risch (Idaho)

Check this out. The U.S. Hose (…er, that's House) of Representatives also has an ethics committee and all kinds of rulebooks at the following website:

http://ethics.house.gov/Pubs/Default.aspx

Available from the House Ethics websites…
2008 House Ethics Manual
Highlights of the House Ethics Rules (PDF Document)
Code of Official Conduct
Committee Rules

Alinsky's point was no one can abide by all the rules all the time. Everyone breaks the rules at least by accident, but these bozos have broken every ethical rule Americans value. It's time for a little payback. This includes the Republicans who have refused to stand up for us. You could have expected the current Democrat-controlled congress to execute on Obama's agenda and the media to cheerlead it. The surprise was the Republican complicity in all this. The worst is what they have done to each other.

I have watched Republican presidential nominees for decades tear each other apart like Mesopotamian Sodomites, both before and after the elections. And the entire time, the Democrats sit there and take copious notes on every piece of dirt and laundry in the Republican camp, laughing hysterically as they use the information to elect more sock-puppets for Socialism. The National Education Association has so dumbed.down American schools that the people in Minnesota don't even blink when they have a Senate race won by more votes than they had registered voters.

How is it during a world-wide war with Muslim terrorists a so-called rigorous news industry mindlessly accepts (indeed declares off-limits the subject of) a presidential candidate's Muslim past until he is elected and speaking before a large Muslim audience in Egypt; and then the same somnambulistic media-outlets applaud him for his mystical Muslim rapport with the enemy? How is it that an administration that runs on "transparency" and a pledge to provide at least five days of public review for new legislation drives unprinted and unread congressional bills to passage that will require the tax-enslavement of three generations of Americans? How is it that during the coolest summer June month in the history of keeping weather records the three stooges in Washington have the nerve to present a congressional bill on global warming? How is it these intellectual diatoms can present a 'Cap and Trade' bill as a job-saver when any freshman economics student could tell you it is a job-killer. Alinsky thought corporations corrupt; they were pikers compared to the magnitude of this politically motivated organized crime.

The vehicle of this fraud is and always has been taxation. From the time the English Crown levied taxes against the colonists until the coercive specialists in Washington D.C. drove through the generational "stimulus" protection racket passed this year, taxes have been the lifeblood of Socialism.  Recently I received an email from a friend (one of those 'please send this to everyone you know' things) and it contained the following list of taxes enacted in just the last one hundred years...

*Accounts Receivable Tax*
*Building Permit Tax*
*CDL license Tax*
*Cigarette Tax*
*Corporate Income Tax*
*Dog License Tax*
*Excise Taxes*
*Federal Firearms License Tax*
*Federal Firearms (Title II) Transfer Tax*
*Federal Income Tax*
*Federal Unemployment Tax (FUTA)*
*Fishing License Tax*
*Food License Tax*
*Fuel Permit Tax*
*Gasoline Tax (currently 44.75 cents per gallon)*
*Gross Receipts Tax*
*Hunting License Tax*
*Inheritance Tax*
*Inventory Tax*
*Liquor Tax*
*Luxury Taxes*
*Marriage License Tax*
*Medicare Tax*
*Personal Property Tax*
*Pitman-Robertson Conservation Tax*
*Property Tax*
*Real Estate Tax*
*Service Charge T ax*
*Social Security Tax*
*Road Usage Tax*

*Sales Tax*
*Recreational Vehicle Tax*
*School Tax*
*State Income Tax*
*State Unemployment Tax (SUTA)*
*Telephone Federal Excise Tax*
*Telephone Federal Universal Service Fee Tax*
*Telephone Federal, State and Local Surcharge Taxes*
*Telephone Minimum Usage Surcharge=2 0Tax*
*Telephone Recurring and Non-recurring Charges Tax*
*Telephone State and Local Tax*
*Telephone Usage Charge Tax*
*Transportation Highway Tax*
*Utility Taxes*
*Vehicle License Registration Tax*
*Vehicle Sales Tax*
*Watercraft Registration Tax*
*Well Permit Tax*
*Workers Compensation Tax*

This last week I heard that New York City officials have proposed raising taxes on their 1700 wealthiest families to an incredible 60% tax rate. Even FDR's congress balked at 50%. If NYC thinks they have a tax shortage now, wait until these 1700 families move to another state with more rational tax rates. As my friend Dr. Terry Lovell repeatedly tells people, "...Socialism always fails when it runs out of everyone else's money."

Probably the biggest fraud in Socialist tax history is the Waxman-Markey "Cap and Trade" legislation currently being rammed down our constituent throats. *The Wall Street Journal* on June 26, 2009 called this the "...biggest tax in American history." The idea is that the Federal Government through coercion (a.k.a. taxation) will first set an arbitrary limit on the amount of carbon emissions emitted into the atmosphere; then through a license/permit system collect tax revenues for those emissions. Then the thumb-screw begins...over time the government starts lowering the acceptable limit (the cap).

> *"The hit to GDP is the real threat in this bill. The whole point of cap and trade is to hike the price of electricity and gas so that Americans will use less. These higher prices will show up not just in electricity bills or at the gas station but in every manufactured good, from food to cars. Consumers will cut back on spending, which in turn will cut back on production, which results in fewer jobs created or higher unemployment. Some companies will instead move their operations overseas, with the same result."*
>
> *Wall Street Journal, 6-26-2009*

This legislative sleight of hand is what passes for Obama's goofball approach to political change in Washington. In fact, the entire carbon emissions hoax which this bill is based upon is so fraudulent it would take another book and a Tolstoy imagination to begin debunking it. It is a perfect ruse for the Socialist agenda; destroy the critical thinking skills of average Americans and then foist enormous technological frauds of legislation on the public ("...a problem so big only the government can solve..."); legislation that produces no change but for the worse and pushes generations of accumulated wealth to the criminal politicians to promote further Socialist agenda items.

Last night I watched the O'Reilly Factor and Bill O'Reilly was popping a vein in his head over the money Goldman Sachs was going to make on the Waxman Markey legislation. You can scream like O'Reilly about the profits, but in the end it is the Obama Socialist agenda legislatively impregnating the U.S. Congress with the Rosemary's Baby of economics that sets the stage for this payoff.

The more wealth is drained from the taxpayer and redistributed initially to the welfare recipient and the politician, the poorer all of us become. The Republicans only get this half-right. They usually say the wealthy will become poorer and the poor will be rewarded; in fact *the poor become poorer*. And yet, in their ignorance and the increasing poverty of Socialist control the poor continue to rise up and re-elect every Socialist hack that tells them the BIG LIE about Socialism and the phony Utopia it pretends to promise.

Personally, I am tired of people being "nice" about Socialism and the petty criminals they run for office. I just don't suffer fools the way I used to. Being nice got us here…I believe to succeed in this battle of wills we must now take the gloves off. Alinsky's fifth rule was to ridicule an opponent's most potent weapon. Ridicule is an ugly weapon which is why it works. Ugly sticks like skunk stink. We need to make Socialism so revoltingly ugly that every time it shows its zit-face in public, people are revolted by it.

This must begin with a bellwether change in the way we think. It is bad enough that most of the mainstream media operates as professional cheerleaders for Socialism and only Fox News offers a microscopically small alternative to what passes for objective journalism. What is far worse is most of us are not really on the program. We have all suffered through too many years of academic diatribe on First Amendment freedoms; how wonderful America is that we can discuss any topic no matter how strange or foreign. We are told this is what makes us free. Fair enough, except this is not a conversation between two wide-eyed students having an academic discussion. It's about the future of the free world.

I am here to say there is a big difference between advocating first amendment protections for open discussion of diverse opinions and hiding behind the amendment in order to perpetrate the destruction of Capitalism and American liberty. The foundations of America are in jeopardy here and we continue to allow the perversion of state-sponsored Socialism at the price of our own peril.

I'm just going to say it right out…Socialism is treason. Socialism is criminally motivated political terrorism. Both terrorism and treason are anathema to liberty and those who advocate it are political criminals. This is not complicated. Barack Hussein Obama, Harry Reid and Nancy Pelosi are traitors. Left unbridled they will continue to destroy the liberty it has taken mankind millennia to create.

Clear-thinking Americans must begin to view Socialism as a prosecutable crime and recognize those who conspire to advance it are in fact criminals to be adjudicated in courts of Federal law. We must embrace the notion our Founding Fathers defined high crimes because they are real, they being perpetrated against America and they need to be prosecuted.

There are people who say we can't play Alinsky's dirty game and if we do our ethics have been compromised in the process and we have lost by definition; today these people are legion. News flash...as of November 2008 we lost America to the Socialists and we lost it because we were unwilling to hit below the belt when we had the chance. There is no compromise in combat and this is combat, make no mistake about it; as in the defense of our homes, our families and our lives, those who would promote quiet, passive resistance are either innocents who have never been in a real fight, are ignoring the realities of combat, or are part of the conspiracy to destroy you.

You cannot negotiate with the unwavering intent of evil.

I listened recently to Michael Steele, selected this last year as the leader of the Republican Party, who said we can still win this battle and win it ethically with our heads held high. I know Steel means well, I do not doubt his patriotic conviction, his conservative commitment nor his intent to win elections. The problem is on this issue he is full of political shit. This is not a fight sanctioned by the Marquess of Queensbury rules. Steele thinks he can hold his head up while the Socialistas kick us in the balls? It doesn't work like that. It's now June, 2009. We're six months into the largest theft of wealth and liberty in the history of the world and the GOP website still has its 2008 "Loser" platform available for immediate download. My question is "...what year are you guys operating in?"

During the American Revolution George Washington listened patiently as the Michael Steele's of colonial times pondered the tactics of gentlemanly dissent, rational thought and logical debate as the King of England proceeded at his convenience to relieve the colonies of their wealth, their dignity and their cherished liberty.

Finally, Washington and others became bored with this approach to the quietly reasoned debate regarding the rape of America, recognized tax-slavery as a historical crime against all humanity, and dutifully picked up a rifle and started shooting British soldiers.

Unaware of it, but having identified the enemy, Washington proceeded to use several other Alinsky tactics to his advantage; "...keep the pressure up; hit them and then hit them again"; outmanned and outgunned he found "...the threat is more terrifying than the thing itself," and "...Power is not only what you have but what the enemy thinks you have"; and finally "...in a fight almost anything goes."

It is at this point the enemies of liberty, and in particular the prostituted minions of the mainstream media, begin to label any First Amendment protected discussion of tax revolt and other forms of activism as potential red-neck psychotic violence, or in the words of Janet Napolitano, we are "...dangerous, right-wing extremists."

Thank you very much; I'm ok with that. I am quite happy for the Socialists to think of us as dangerous. These cheap political sluts should be afraid...they should be very afraid. While I oppose any use of violence to solve purely political issues, I have no problem with good people breaking the law in order to break the back of Socialism. These political criminals are the enemy of freedom, they have no respect for the rule of law themselves and have already bent or completely broken U.S. Constitutional frameworks in order to confiscate, redistribute and tax the wealth of hard-working Americans for decades to come. The Tea Parties across America demonstrate that people are waking up to this, they are angry about it and they are motivated to end this irrational decimation of liberty.

Let me be clear; after the Islamic extremists brought terror to our shores on 9-11, their political allies and apologists lurking inside America conspired to bring this treason to the White House and to Congress. There is no Constitutional authority for instituting this psychotic agenda of collectivist state-sponsored Socialism, just as there is no enumerated government right to control and manipulate businesses nor banks nor the automotive industry. And finally, any argument that government coercion foisted on the American people in order to control either the economy or the climate or health care is intellectual and moral fraud by definition. The political whores of Washington are in the process of burning the Constitution and they will burn the deed to your home and the title to your business, they will destroy your birthright and enslave your children and grandchildren with taxes and, if necessary, if they cannot get the clergy's ecumenical complicity they will burn the Bible to get what they want.

We did not ask for this fight, but we will not walk quietly away from it.

In the next and final chapter I am going to share with you some very dangerous information. Properly used it will strike fear into the heart of Socialism, put freedom back into the mainstream of America and restore Capitalism as the great economic engine of liberty it was meant to be.

The only thing we need is to have you on the program.

# Part V: Just Desserts

*"The revolution is not an apple that falls when it is ripe. You have to make it fall."*
—Ernesto 'Che' Guevara [13]

## No Good Deed Goes Unpunished

Che's inventive interpretation of Newtonian physics in not without the sort of social irony that would have been appreciated by Sir Newton. Guevara was amidst all things a pragmatic warrior who kept his nose to the revolutionary grindstone in much the same way Newton went after the mysteries of the universe. Regrettably, like Alinsky, Che fought for the right reasons on the wrong side and in the end he paid the ultimate price. We will wish to avoid doing the same. However, there are lessons from the revolutionary left that can be learned from Che and a few other notable nut cases that can benefit our activist sojourn in turning the tables on Socialism.

Complicating this particular discussion of revolutionary tactics traditionally used by committed leftists will be the Biblical gremlin of temptation. A great deal of what has been done to us by the political criminals in general and to America in particular makes us angry; and it should. Col. Jeff Cooper, who was one of my mentors in life, used to say that getting angry was a good thing. You can channel anger toward an opponent in combat, and use that emotion to defeat them even if you have no other weapon. But Cooper tried to beat it into us that you had to channel that anger *before* you went into combat; you had to place yourself in that situation prior to someone else putting you there and you must make a decision on what you were going to do before you have to do it. This sort of "pre-cognitive imaging for success" is something firearms instructors and athletic coaches have routinely taught self-defense clients and successful athletes for decades.

It's called planning ahead. There is an old adage in the martial arts community that those who win, study the fight before it begins; everyone else fights first and then studies why they lost.

Without planning, without thoughtful, committed reasoned consideration to planning and organization we are doing little more than becoming a reckless legend in our own minds. Worse, without planning, the great human urge to temptation, to improvise without rational thought, quickly approaches the slippery slope of legality. As you review the material in this section, be careful. Many of the tactics and strategies I presented here are successful and useful but depending on how they are implemented can and will reflect your own ethics. Some of these tactics were illegally implemented by people who were operating with government supplied "get out of jail free cards" or were outside the law themselves and had nothing to lose.

> *"Those who walk as though they are in Paradise should be very sure that is exactly where they are..."*
> — **Gunsite Gossip,** Jeff Cooper

While you may be morally justified to go outside the law in the interests of defeating Socialism; outlawry carries with it profound penalties, particularly when wielded by irrational national despots, anti-American Attorney Generals, and other local criminals and what Michael Savage calls their sub-human minions. In fact, you should expect that the line of activism which lies between the legal and justifiable activities of free speech and the darker side of our combined and justifiable desperation will be purposefully blurred by the criminal lawmakers in order to make the First Amendment more and more inaccessible as time goes by; particularly as we begin to be successful with our legal actions.

These cretins have just committed the largest transfer of wealth in the history of the world; they think nothing of lying, cheating, or stealing. Why, when confronted with legal protest, do you think they would suddenly find ethical behavior to be their new path? Consider that once hit, our opponents may and probably will make the aftermath of the situation look worse than we made it in order to create the prosecutable illusion of illegality. Use the techniques of stealth to protect you and your people from falling into the trap of expecting them to follow ethical rules.

Frankly, a strict interpretation of Alinsky's rules of power politics falls squarely into the realm of conspiracy. While many, if not most of Wild Bill Donovan's tactics from World War II were excused as the ethics of prosecuting a just war, they are none the less the psychological warfare tools of highly illegal military sabotage and espionage. While I will also refer to some of Dave Foreman's strategies from his controversial book on Monkeywrenching; please note he went to jail. Foreman leveraged traditional labor tactics against industrial and corporate entities he considered anti-environmental. If you don't include the jail time, he was very successful. There is great stuff here, but you must be careful with it. Our primary objective is breaking the back of Socialism, not going to jail.

> *"Espionage is not a nice thing, nor are the*
> *methods employed exemplary...we face an*
> *enemy who believes one of his chief weapons is*
> *that none but he will employ terror..."*
> —Wild Bill Donovan

At Alinsky's invitation, let us employ our imaginations. There are well-honed tools of activism from which we can draw both experience and data. Whether you intend to operate alone or with friends, you will find time is against you. When I was at Intel Corporation, a common saying was "...work smarter, not harder". Let's look at some of the tools available to save you some time.

## Public Records Research

Thorough research cannot be overstated. The government leaves paper trails like slugs leave goo. Public records can be a gold mine of information both in terms of alerts to government action as well as evidentiary material to legal proceedings, but mining that data can be arduous and gaining access to it can be challenging. In 1974 the Freedom of Information Act (FOIA) was passed by Congress with the understanding that the law "...is based upon the presumption that the government and the information of government belong to the people." Alinsky's fourth rule of power tactics was to make the enemy live up to their own book of rules. The FOIA is one such rule book. Currently the Department of Justice maintains a website with a compilation of contacts for everyone in the government who handles FOIA requests and is categorized by agency. This site is currently located at: http://www.usdoj.gov/oip/foiacontacts.htm.

It is important to understand that there is no central office in the government which processes FOIA requests for all federal agencies. Each agency responds to requests for its own records. Therefore, before sending a request, you should determine whether the agency you are contacting is likely to have the records you are seeking. Other general sources of information about how to make a FOIA request include: "Your Right to Federal Records," available for fifty cents per copy from the Consumer Information Center, Department 319E, Pueblo, CO 81009. This publication also can be accessed electronically at:
http://www.pueblo.gsa.gov/cic_text/fed_prog/foia/foia.htm

"A Citizen's Guide on Using the Freedom of Information Act and the Privacy Act of 1974 to Request Government Records." This report is published by the Committee on Government Reform and Oversight of the House of Representatives. It is available for sale for $5.00 from the U.S. Government Printing Office, stock number 052-071-01230-3. It also can be accessed on the World Wide Web at:
http://www.tncrimlaw.com/foia_indx.html

At the federal level of government are all sorts of information holdings that can be useful. The Federal Communications Commission (FCC) requires and catalogs information from companies and individuals involved in licensed television, radio, and cable TV stations. For instance, the FCC can provide information on La Network Campesina, a radio station which is part of a larger network of stations supporting illegal immigration (http://www.campesina.com), and is one of the most rampant border anarchist broadcasters here in Arizona. La Network Campesina is a huge network which grew out of the Corky Gonzales farm workers movement.

Other federal resources for research include the Federal Reserve Board (located on the web at http://www.federalreserve.gov) , National Labor Relations Board (http://www.nlrb.gov), and the Federal Energy Regulatory Commission (http://www.ferc.gov). Contributions to federal elections are recorded and available from the Federal Elections Commission (http://www.fec.gov). Presidential candidates must also file contribution information in the states where they spend money. Candidates typically have campaign committees which must also divest themselves of information through public record, usually available from your Secretary of State Office. Congressional directories reveal who is lobbying in Washington, again available through Worldcat.org at your library or purchase online. Personal finances of US Senators are filed with the Secretary of the Senate, Office of Public Records (SOPR at http://www.senate.gov). Lobbyists also register with the Senate Office of Public Records in accordance with the Lobbying Disclosure Act (LDA). Lobbying and other records are available for public inspection. On the federal House of Representatives side is the House Committee on Standards of Official Conduct (http://ethics.house.gov).

## Grass Roots

You will find a great deal of information regarding a wide range of subjects at your local county recorder's office. The recorder's office does just what it sounds like; records documents, as required by law, which are part of the public record. Documents recorded include real estate transactions, mortgages, deeds of trust, family trusts, personal property, tax liens, mining locations, subdivision plats, records of survey, military discharges, official appointments of office, and other documents required to be made of public record. Many of these documents will be available in paper form, or in the case of earlier historic records may be available in microfilm. Here in Arizona, by legislative statute the Recorder's Office is also in charge of Voter Registration (get those voter registration forms from these guys).

Our county government also has an extensive Global Information System (GIS) with digital mapping of our entire county including overlays of property and not only who owns the property but who owned back into recorded history (I'm not kidding). These systems can be correlated to embarrassing back-tax information and sale of property for non-payment of taxes. The GIS is available to the public via an internet website which also offers the entire county agency service network. Both street and rural mapping information is incredibly useful when planning activism.

Other local agencies are also capable of providing you with useful data. Alinsky's thirteenth rule of power politics was "...pick the target, freeze it, *personalize it*, and polarize it". In many cases you will be looking for personal information on individuals. The local coroner's office may be able to provide data on relatives of deceased citizens; spousal and maternal maiden names are two of the most common aliases. Salary, job title, tenure, retirement benefits and sometimes work history of government employees are listed with various civil service agencies, personnel departments or state comptroller's office. You can really create havoc with an individual by simply knowing where they work and calling their personnel office pretending to be an employer who has received their application for a job; that little zinger will go back to their boss about thirty seconds after you hang up (don't forget to use a public phone). This is called social engineering.

Don't forget the newspaper. Local, county and state law enforcement agencies routinely place arrest information in the newspapers (the big arrests make it on local radio). New corporations are required to place public announcements in the newspaper; business licenses while not necessarily incorporated also appear in the paper. The obits are full of data.

When it comes to individuals, you will eventually bump up against privacy laws, many of which were enacted at about the same time as the FOIA. A useful library text on this subject is the *Compilation of State and Federal Privacy Laws* available in many public libraries. If you want one for your own reference it is available on Amazon.com (where else?). The current version was published in 2002 and contains a 2009 Supplement (ISBN 0-930072-17-0) (new 13-digit ISBN: 9780930072179).

If you don't have a library card, you are missing the whole point on information. A very valuable reference in the library is called *Business Information Sources.* Now published by the University of California Press and in its third edition (October 12, 1993) you may also order this reference online and in good used condition can sell for only a couple of bucks (ISBN-10: 0520081803 / ISBN-13: 978-0520081802). It not only contains information on how to use libraries as research vehicles for information but includes important information on time-saving resources and specific information on finding information on corporations, organizations, businesses and individuals, and industrial research. Libraries also typically keep a copy of *Standard and Poor's Register of Corporations, Directors and Executive*, as well as *Dunn and Bradstreet Directories*. Libraries also have enormous inter-library resources. Your local and state court system will also have public records on arrests, convictions, divorce, law suits, criminal records, and probate. Inheritance, particularly property is often run through probate procedures and includes name and address information on everyone concerned.

# Field Tactics

*"When the forces of oppression come to maintain themselves in power against established law, peace is already considered broken..."*
### Guerrilla Warfare—1961
Che Guevara [13]

Bear in mind, the anarchists and political criminals beat us at this game and they are now mostly aging pony-tailed pot-smoking anarcho-pacifists; beat them with their own stick. They created the tax oppression necessary for this beating to occur; we need only enough motivation to actually pick up the stick and do what needs doing. Much of what needs to be done can occur in our local communities (political rallies, voter registration drives, political activism, etc.). A lot of initial work must be done right now; organizing and recruiting are vital. This is not as hard as it might sound; a lot of people already are completely outraged by what is going on and clearly see the futility in further inaction. Direct that anger.

We need to recognize just because Obama and his criminal organization hold the power of both government and law enforcement, this does not mean we are powerless. In fact, in many ways, diverse local action has an advantage over large slow-moving bureaucracies. Guevara detailed this in an analysis of the Mao revolution in China where initial failures were overcome when the movement finally took up a rural base and made agrarian land reform their fundamental goal. It is always about the land and the wealth it represents. From the French fiat money fiasco of the 1700's to Ho Chi Minh's peasant rebellion to the Arab-French Algerian conflict, it is about who gets the wealth of the land for their own use. As Obama begins his nationalization of American wealth, our freedom to own property and to control our individual destiny through that private ownership is now at risk. What are you willing to do?

Please note: don't physically hurt _anybody_ in the process. Unlike totalitarian civilizations where any warm body will do, in America every life is valuable and this even includes people who have been directed against us by the media, or poor education, politics or bad upbringing. The measure of our ultimate success is the whole world on the program for liberty. It's a big job.

Several obvious field tactics are necessary; secretiveness about our actions contribute to our ability to leverage surprise actions and as indicated earlier protects our people; legal but ruthless treachery disorients the opposition and disrupts their crime; repeated action divides and overcomes their organizational and operational ability; and Alinsky's eighth rule of power tactics "...keep the pressure up". Hit them, hit them again, and then hit them again. The target should not be allowed to sleep thinking all is well. During an action the target must believe they are completely surrounded even if they are not (remember Alinsky's ninth rule of power tactics "...the threat is usually more terrifying than the thing itself"). To do this successfully you must have an objective ("...pick the target"), you must then analyze the target in terms of resistance (how big is the target in terms of people, building size or location), how mobile are they, who are their leaders and how affective is their leadership likely to be when pressed into confrontation?

### *Plan the Action*

Having determined these things, you now plan the specific action. It is necessary to determine in the beginning whether this is to be a planned public action with pre-press publicity (don't forget to get the permits), or a hit and run strike. In either event, it is imperative that you and/or your organization are not compromised before, during or after the action. Political and organizational survival is the key thing; you must live to fight another day even when you are faced with failure. Comedian Bob Newhart planned every standup routine he had by building upon the previous punch line in what appeared to be an improvisational continuum of off-hand punch lines; but at each point if the continuum did not appear to be working he had an exit line that allowed him to move easily to a new line of humor. Always have multiple exit plans prepared for each phase of an action including a bailout in the beginning if things clearly are not coming together. You need to know who is driving and who's riding. An important aspect of both planning and exit strategies are the use of good maps, know where you are going, have an alternate route and run all routes in practice runs ahead of time. Take photographs ahead of time if necessary and use them to help visualize what you are going to do. Local organizational resources can be useful here as well; knowing individuals who live or work in the area can provide a temporary and immediate location to get you and your people off the street in a hurry in the case of weather or other problems.

### *Eyes and ears...*

Unless you are operating alone and performing very small actions or planning reconnaissance for future events, the larger actions always require eyes on the street to be looking out for you. The more watchers you have the more likely you will not be surprised by response from the target.

This includes having eyes on the entry and exit routes as well as eyes on the event. It is not unlikely you may run across other people or groups who are actually in the process of committing illegal activities (burglary, illegal dumping, etc.); at that point you need to bail out and call the cops.

While cell phones can be useful in communicating with your activists, the ubiquitous CB radio is a better choice as you can have multiple people online at the same time. Place your people in position for practice communication runs; be sure the radios can work from the actual locations; be sure everyone has new batteries on the day of the event and backup batteries in their pockets. If possible, have backup radios. Have pre-prepared codes that do not "announce" what you are doing to the target and the rest of the world.

## Dress for Success

When your action is semi-covert, perhaps to reconnoiter information at the target location, you and your people should wear clothing that allows them to blend in. In rural Arizona you blend with a cowboy hat; in Chicago a cowboy hat is going to stick out like a silk suit at a rodeo. Wearing locally branded sports merchandise can be useful (how about some Obama-branded stuff?), but I think clothing that has absolutely *no advertising on it at all* is the best choice. Sunglasses are always helpful, wigs provide complete misdirection. Blue jeans, a ball cap, sneakers and a hoodie can be pretty inconspicuous unless you are in a corporate environment where dressy casual or ties are the norm. Conform and disappear; stick out and fail.

If necessary, have a different set of clothes available for changing after the targeted action is complete. Have one set of clothes for use at the event, and another after you have made the exit. Have a place and a method for stashing both. Gloves are mandatory in most cases; the cheap cotton ones won't break your heart to throw away and are easily replaced. If you need to use the tight fitting latex shop gloves remember, they leave a nice set of your fingerprints inside the glove; be sure to take them with you and destroy them by melting.

Hats are useful, particularly for warmth in the winter or in the summer for portable shade. However, remove the labels, avoid branding information that can identify you, and don't wear great big hats that can snag or hang up on overhanging trees, window entries, or low-hanging office decorations. Picking things up that fall off of you is a waste of time and if you lose them the item becomes evidence.

You can be traced by your shoes; use either cheap sneakers that you can throw away after the action is over (consider oversize shoes with extra socks) or large socks worn over the shoes to conceal the tread. Avoid the plastic grocery store bags as they will not hold up to even light use. Wear long sleeved shirts and do not wear shorts; try to have everything covered somehow. Do not wear loose fitting clothes that can potentially snag and leave behind threads or torn swatches.

### *What Time is It?*

Mobility and timing are critical. As your plan emerges it will be necessary to create schedules that must be adhered to on a minute basis, sometimes down to the second. Diversionary tactics are always good and can be used effectively to draw attention away from where you are actually doing something important. Hunters know moving animals (which present a more difficult shot) can be immobilized momentarily by yelling at the animal. Amazingly they do not run away but stop and look at the yelling hunter and that is when he takes his shot. People are the same, if you present a ruckus on one side of building, the occupants will all go to the windows on that side of the building to look, and at that point...you go in the back door. Keeping the pressure on, you then create another ruckus, perhaps on another side of the building or in the building itself that creates a diversion for your exit.

### *Identify Vulnerabilities*

In creating diversions or any other action, it is important to identify vulnerabilities in the target that can be leveraged to your advantage. Poor security, slack-jawed employees, unattended phones, somnambulistic work routines, unattended computers, empty office or storage space, unlocked vehicles, unfenced commercial yards, easily copied uniforms or identification badges are all useful vulnerabilities; use your imagination. What they are doing to our communities makes the vulnerable. Exploit the tactics they use, the events they sponsor, the groups who support them; everybody has something to hide, your job is find out what they don't want you to know.

### *Tools*

As an engineer this is a subject near and dear to my heart. While the mind is the backbone of activism; tools can help facilitate what the mind conceives. I was once asked in a robotics job interview what I thought might be my most important tool. Cleverly, I said "...my mind." True enough, but if you need to make some holes in wood, a drill gun is a better choice than your head. Remember anything with iron in it can and will rust. If you are storing tools be sure they are oiled and in at least damp-proof locations or plastic bags with moisture absorbing bags. If you are buying specific tools remember to pay cash and buy them out of town. Be sure to remove any store specific identification tags or labels. If possible, buy things at large stores like Wal-Mart, Target, etc. or at flea markets or yard sales where both you and your purchase will blend in with the crowd. For any particular action, break up the purchases and buy some at one outlet, the rest somewhere else.

For the most part, your plan will dictate what tools will help accomplish your goal. Spend enough to be sure they will work, but remember you may have to dump them; designer tools do nothing for you. Have enough tools for the job; standing around waiting for a screwdriver is a waste of everyone's time, increases security problems and creates scheduling issues. Whatever tools you use, have a separate set of tools for activism from your tools at home. Most tools are capable of leaving tool marks that are identifiable. Never take your activist tools home; have a good, dry, easily accessible stash for them. The list below is not that expensive and can be purchased for under $50.

I have already mentioned clothing and CB radios (don't forget the batteries). Pocket knives are always helpful, firearms are not. Other useful and basic items for any activity from rallies to political benefits...

| | |
|---|---|
| • Super Glue<br>• Spray Paint<br>• Upholstery Staple Gun<br>• Gorilla Tape<br>• Water<br>• Leatherman<br>• Rope | • First Aid Kit<br>• Eye protection<br>• Hammer<br>• Screwdriver<br>• Socket set<br>• Side cutters<br>• Adjustable Wrench |

Moving tools from storage to the target needs to be considered. Organizing your tools in a tool belt is always advised but wearing it into a place of business may not be the best choice. I know people who have packed machine guns into brightly colored diaper bags and no one in Starbucks knew the difference. Backpacks and belly packs are everywhere these days and can also provide useful transportation. Military ammo cans can be excellent for storage and nearly waterproof if in good condition, but add unnecessary weight when transporting. Only take what you need, nothing more, and nothing less.

### Psy-Ops

It is all psychological. Use your head, be creative. Your personal computer and printer/scanner can be enormously useful. Create your own invitations to gala parties offering FREE dinners hosted by your favorite criminal politician. Schedule your invitees to show up at the same location and time he is having a $100/plate benefit. If they are having a big phone bank activity or public event, infiltrate the event and put a stink bomb in the room. Any public appearance is an opportunity for a whipped cream pie in the face.

*Silent agitators* were effectively used by Dave Foreman's Earth First! organization and documented in his radical book on Eco-Terrorism called *Ecodefense* [12]. These are small decal or sticker labels with a recognizable graphic representing the revolution. Foreman indicated this tradition goes back to the early 1900's with the International Workers of the World movement (IWW or Wobblies as they were then known). An iconic graphic with a short and sweet message can be used to flaunt your message in conspicuous places.

The goal is for your target and your action to come together in the minds of the public as a justifiable deed and clearly recognizable as blow for American liberty. When the public is on your side you are winning the revolution, expanding opportunity for new recruits, and creating justification for the necessary havoc to decimate Socialism.

Always remember: truth, justice and the American way are on your side.

# *Epilogue...*

> *"It is vain to summon a people, which has been rendered so dependent on the central power, to choose from time to time the representatives of that power; this rare and brief exercise of this free choice... however important it may be, will not prevent them from gradually losing the faculties of thinking, feeling, and acting for themselves, and thus gradually falling below the level of humanity."*
>
> **Democracy in America**—1835,
> Alexis de Tocqueville

De Tocqueville knew something of economic self-destruction; he had watched this irrational theater of the absurd unfold in France just a few short years before he wrote those words; the grotesque and twisted images of broken lives and human corpses were very fresh in his mind. They too had seen it coming, and could not stop the self-annihilation of an entire nation. Once the political criminals got their hands on the printing presses that controlled production of a fiat money system, like a clueless heroin addict in a dirty little alley, they could not stop themselves.

Like Obama, they nationalized the banks; then using the banks as a complicit vehicle of their madness, they confiscated church property and sold the sacred real estate with bank loans given to dubious borrowers using the inflated paper currency. The economic disaster was only the beginning. After that came the insane rationalizations of failure that inevitably accompanies the sociopath psychosis of political vampires. Returning again and again to the failed inflationary spigot of fiat money production to supply the French royals and the sycophant elite with opulent luxury; unable to accept blame for the very act that was destroying the nation's economy, they turned their guilt on their own labor force. First dissenters were vilified, then beheaded, and then the rigors of despotism were visited on everyone. As the guillotines began to run red with the blood of the innocent and guilty alike, and the Bastille overflowed as all totalitarian fear state prisons must, the intellectual serenity, individual liberty, great art, and leadership that once was called the French Enlightenment became a degenerating national nightmare historically known as *The Reign of Terror*. Before it was over, many of France's best and brightest craftsmen, artists, engineers and business owners were destroyed economically, beheaded, or driven from the country. Two hundred years later, France has yet to recover from this humanitarian deficit.

If you don't think America is headed there, think again. Absolutely drunk with power, Obama and his thugs have begun to nationalize the banking system while printing presses of the Federal Reserve run reams of fiat currency at full tilt boogie to finance the greatest Socialist financial fraud in history. And while President Obama laughs—a journalist at the annual correspondent's dinner in May 2009 proposes the joyful death of a conservative dissenter, Speaker Nancy Pelosi flies high above both responsibility and a broken economy in a government supplied jet at taxpayer expense. Harry Reed, the original mental midget, plots the next perverse redirection of guilt (anywhere but at himself), and Treasury Secretary Tim Geithner plans the financial redistribution of all American wealth.

We are only as free as the freedoms we exercise, it is time to make the government listen to the people again; it is time to rekindle the freedom America was born for; it is time to give our children and our grandchildren the liberty our forefathers died for. From the mayor's office to the state legislature, to congress and the White House, it is time to kick some Socialist butt.

Right now...this minute as you read this, is unquestionably America's most urgent hour. The last time anything else was remotely as important was the American Declaration of Independence. The time has come to make a choice. Would you like to have Obama reserve you a chair on the People's Thought Farm? Or, can we count on you to help break the chain of political and social crime gripping American politics?

America as we have known it is out of time...time for you to decide.

.

# Appendix A:
## *SOME SUGGESTED RADICAL TARGETS*

<u>ACORN</u>: Association of Community Organizers for Reform Now. One of the most visible community-based voter registration frauds, ACORN has been the subject of repeated expose. ACORN was formed from the old National Welfare Rights Organization who sought in the 1960's to eliminate all restrictions to getting welfare money. In 2008, ACORN members and staff knocked on the doors of hundreds of thousands of low-income and working neighborhoods to make contact with potential voters. Voter registration crews also target high traffic areas like shopping centers and grocery stores, and special events like street festivals, sporting events, naturalization ceremonies and hip-hop concerts. ACORN International has changed its name to **Community Organizers International** (COI). As of this writing (June 2009) the name change only affects ACORN International. However it is rumored that ACORN (domestic) will change their name as well due to all the negative press. There may be other changes soon to follow. Website last found at: http://www.acorn.org

<u>Black Radical Congress</u>: Left-wing coalition of African-American activists formed in 1998 in East St. Louis. This broad confederation seeks to increase radicalism among the Blacks of America, and specifically denounces Black Capitalists. The BRC has numerous caucuses which seek to promote such left-wing goals as trade unionism, feminism, gay and youth rights, and (specifically) an end to the incarceration of Mumia Abu-Jamal. BRC national headquarters is located in New York. Website found at: http://www.blackradicalcongress.org/

<u>Committees of Correspondence for Democracy and Socialism</u>: This group was formed after the Soviet coup of 1991 by Manning Marable, Carl Boice, Leslie Cagan, Charlene Mitchell, Angela Davis, Pete Seeger and numerous others who were expelled from (or left) the Communist Party for supporting Mikhail Gorbachev and the pro-democracy faction of the Russian government. Free of the CPUSA, the CCDS founders hoped to unite the divided American Left, and received support from a number of well-known leftists,

including Noam Chomsky. However, this dream soon ran into the classic problem of sectarianism, and CCDS floundered. Over the years, the political alignment of CCDS shifted dramatically, from its infancy in Reform Communism to become a democratic Socialist organization, not very different from DSA or the Socialist Party USA. Website sometimes found at:  http://www.cofc.org/

**Communist Party USA:** Formed in Chicago 1919 as two Leninist splinters from the Socialist Party of America: the Communist Party of America (CPA) and the Communist Labor Party (CLP). Both groups had supported Vladimir Lenin, the Bolsheviks and the new Soviet Union, but were different demographically (the CPA was mostly composed of immigrants and the native-born CLP was lead by journalist John Reed). Lenin's Communist International ("Comintern") forced these two groups to merge in order to become the official American section of the Comintern. The CPA and CLP merged in 1922 to become the United Communist Party and later the Workers (Communist) Party (WCP).  Though experiencing a new growth, the CP-USA still supports a number of views, such as calling the current Chinese government "Socialist" in their journals and backing the Colombian FARC. The Communist Party publishes a newspaper (*People's Weekly World*) and a magazine (*Political Affairs*). Website found at: http://www.cpusa.org/

**Democratic National Party:** Once merely the liberal voice to balance conservative thought, the DNC leadership has been taken over by Socialists. Perceiving themselves to be "...in a critical moment that will reverberate for generations to come. " The oldest fraud perpetrated in modern politics sees surrendering in Iraq, redistribution of wealth, corporate and banking takeovers, and creation of millions of "go-nowhere" jobs, environmental fraud and alternative energies as they way to re-election. No target is larger nor more ripe than these idiots.

**Democratic Socialists of America:** Confederation of Socialists formed in 1983 when a splinter group of the Socialist Party (Michael Harrington's Democratic Socialist Organizing Committee, DSOC) merged with the SDS splinter New American Movement

(NAM). DSA has many celebrity members, including feminist Gloria Steinem, actor Ed Asner, black activist Cornel West, and libertarian Socialist Noam Chomsky. It is also the chief American member group of the Socialist International, which includes the British Labour Party and the French Parti Socialiste. Until just recently, the main aim of DSA was to convert the Democratic Party into a social democratic organization. Also, the current president of the labor federation AFL-CIO, John Sweeney, is also a DSA member. DSA publishes a journal, *Democratic Left*, and has numerous commissions on specific issues, as well as a youth wing (YDS). Though it is still the largest Socialist organization in the US, DSA has been diminishing in size recently. Website found at: http://www.dsausa.org/dsa.html

**Freedom Road Socialist Organization:** Like Solidarity, the group known as Freedom Road was an organization formed by the unification of three smaller groups in 1985 — the Proletarian Unity League, Revolutionary Workers Headquarters, and the Organization for Revolutionary Unity. Though coming from the Maoist tradition, the FRSO began to look more critically at the role of Mao in his later years and the government he left behind. Like Solidarity, Freedom Road also began calling for "Left Refoundation" beyond their traditional segment on the far left — desiring to create a "revolutionary Socialist" organization. In 1999, the pro-Soviet and Stalinist faction broke off to form Freedom Road Socialist Organization (Fight Back) — and affiliated with the hardline Belgian Party of Labour (PTB). FRSO publishes a journal, *Freedom Road Magazine*. Website found at: http://www.freedomroad.org/

**Freedom Socialist Party:** The founders of the FSP were originally the Seattle branch of the Socialist Workers Party. The FSP sought to help blacks through "revolutionary integration," (an idea later adopted by the Spartacist League. The FSP grew beyond Seattle, and eventually made all the way to Canada and Australia. Strongly feminist, internationalist, and supports more modern left-wing causes, including environmentalism, human rights, and gay liberation. The FSP has recently attempted to join the Trotskyist Fourth International (USFI). The FSP publishes a quarterly journal,

*The Freedom Socialist*. The FSP is one of the most active far-left organizations in the Pacific Northwest. Website found at: http://www.socialism.com/

**Green Party:** Founded in July 2001 by the Association of State Green Parties (ASGP) and some supporters of the Greens USA, hoping to establish a strong, unified Green Party in the US following the pathetic success of Green candidate Ralph Nader in 2000 (2.75% in the presidential election). This new GP has formed a National Committee and is seeking recognition from the Federal Elections Commission. Website found at: http://www.gp.org/index.php

**Greens USA:** Environmental organization founded in August of 1991 after much effort to create a success story like the German and French Green parties. For ten years, the G-USA was known as the "Green Party USA." However, in 1996, a moderate GP-USA faction, frustrated that the party's radical politics were not winning converts, formed the Association of State Green Parties (ASGP). After an angry battle for power, the ASGP won, pulling in much more support than the older GP-USA. In the end, the ASGP let the GP-USA join them, but only after they took the "Party" out of their name. The "Greens USA" now serve only as the left wing of the new Green Party. They publish a journal, *Synthesis & Regeneration*. Website found at: http://www.greens.org/

**HuffingtonPost.com:** Predictable internet hate site and blog for America hating morons. Leveraging celebrity status of Greek author Arianna Huffington, the website has been the subject of the vilest Socialist diatribe imaginable.

**Industrial Workers of the World:** The IWW was a radical trade union formed in 1905 by radical Syndicalists and other leftists who opposed the pro-American policies of the American Federation of Labor. "The Wobblies," as the IWW members were called, included many members of the Socialist Party of America, the Socialist Labor Party, and many other radical left-wing groups. The IWW today is more a support group for radical workers than an actual labor union. Website found at: http://www.iww.org/

**International Socialist Organization:** Formed in 1977 by supporters of British theorist Tony Cliff who had instigated a split in Hal Draper's International Socialists. The new ISO, led by Cal and Barbara Wilson, quickly affiliated with the British Socialist Workers Party and its International Socialist Tendency, as well as publishing a newspaper called *Socialist Worker*. Website found at: http://www.internationalSocialist.org/

**Labor Party:** Formed in June 1996 in Cleveland, Ohio, by Adolf Reed's Labor Party Advocates (LPA) — as well as a number of left-leaning unions, including the United Electrical Workers (UE), International Longshoremen (ILWU), American Federation of Government Employees, California Nurses Association, United Mine Workers of America, and numerous locals of other unions. The Labor Party is publishing the bi-monthly *Labor Party Press* and the "Just Health Care" campaign for a national healthcare service. In Wyoming, where the Democrats are weak, the Labor Party also initiated an electoral bloc (a "Blue-Green Alliance") with the Green Party in 1998. The LP has also initiated a think-tank organization, the Debs Jones Douglass Institute. Present national headquarters is in Washington DC. Website found at: http://www.thelaborparty.org/

**League of Revolutionaries for a New America:** Founded in 1968 as the California Communist League by former members of the Communist Party USA. In 1974, the CCL had a national convention and created the "Communist Labor Party" (CLP). The CLP considered themselves traditional Stalinists and Maoists, and opposed the direction that the Communist Party USA was taking by supporting "revisionism" in Russia. They are mostly located in Chicago. Website found at: http://www.lrna.org/index.html

**Left Turn: Notes from the Global Intifada,** A network of activists and organizers committed to social justice (as defined by them) and by publishing *Left Turn* magazine, on www.leftturn.org, and strategizing around the oppressive systems we are trying to tear down and the alternatives we are building. Located primarily in (where else?) New York City and San Francisco. Website found at: http://www.leftturn.org/

**Maoist Internationalist Movement:** A tiny sect of Maoist revolutionaries, formed in October 1983 from an old SDS splinter, "RADACADS." Originally known as the "Revolutionary Internationalist Movement" (RIM), the MIM changed its name in 1984 after the Revolutionary Communist Party took the name RIM for its international organization. Their organization's line also includes right-wing moralist ideas, including homophobia and refusing a woman's right to abortion. Obviously a group of aging New Left cooks, the MIM has only a small clustered membership in Western Massachusetts, Detroit and the Berkeley area. No website information was found.

**MoveOn.org:** A family of organizations made up of a couple of different pieces. MoveOn.org Civic Action was started in 1998 by Joan Blades and Wes Boyd, two Silicon Valley entrepreneurs in an attempt to take the heat off President Bill Clinton's sexual predation. Civic Action is a 501(c)(4) nonprofit organization, formerly known just as MoveOn.org, and primarily focuses on propaganda. MoveOn.org Political Action, a federal PAC, formerly known as MoveOn PAC, mobilizes internet zombies and pinhead phone banks to influence the outcome of congressional elections.

**NAMBLA:** In 1978, after gay activists pounded then-Boston District Attorney Garret Byrne for sting operations intended to arrest teenage male prostitutes (a sex ring of men used drugs and video games to first lure the boys into a house, where they photographed them as they engaged in sexual activity), a meeting of sexual predators and pedophiles was organized at Boston's Community Church. Following that meeting, 34 predators and a number of their brain-dead victims formed the North American Man/Boy Love Association. Website found at: http://www.nambla.org/

**Peace & Freedom Party:** Founded in the 1960's as a left-wing party opposed to the Vietnam War, the PFP reached its peak of support in 1968 when it nominated Black Panther leader Eldridge Cleaver for President. There has been a legal battle (supported by prominent leftists such as Howard Zinn and Noam Chomsky) to get

the PFP back on the California ballot. Website found at:
http://peaceandfreedom.org/home/

**Progressive Labor Party**: Formed in June 1962 in New York as the Progressive Labor Movement by about fifty former members of the Communist Party USA who considered themselves Maoists. The founders of the PLM sympathized with China in what became known as the Sino-Soviet Split — putting them in direct opposition to the CP-USA's "revisionist" line. The PLP took up an anti-revisionist form of Stalinism and supported the "true Socialist" regimes of Albania and North Korea. They are one of the few leftist groups that supports a violent execution of the entire upper class (*à la* Pol Pot's Cambodia). The tiny sect that remains of the PLP exists only in portions of California and New York. They publish a Stalinist newspaper, *Challenge*. Website found at:
http://www.plp.org/

**Revolutionary Communist Party**: Founded as the Bay Area Revolutionary Union (BARU) in the early 1970's by Maoist Bob Avakian. Avakian's Revolutionary Union was one of the factions of Students for a Democratic Society who opposed the Progressive Labor Party. Since 1975, Avakian has created a web of youth/minority/worker protest groups, all quietly commanded by the RCP. The RCP publishes a newspaper, the *Revolutionary Worker*. The RCP also has an international federation, the Revolutionary Internationalist Movement (RIM), which includes the Communist Party (Shining Path) of Peru and the Communist Party of Nepal (Maoist). Chairman Avakian is currently in "exile" in France, hiding from the FBI. Website found at: http://revcom.us/

**Revolutionary Workers League**: Formed in 1976 as a split from the Spartacist League, the RWL is a dogmatic and intensely militant Trotskyist group based in Detroit. Little is seen of them outside of Michigan and California state, and (like the Spartacist League) they demand the devotion of all their members. They have set up a network of puppet organizations: the National Women's Rights Organizing Committee (NWROC, founded 1980's), the Committee to Defend Affirmative Action By Any Means Necessary (BAMN, founded 1995), and others. These front groups are where the

RWL's primary activism takes place. Website found at: http://www.rwl-us.org/ but mostly in Asian language format.

**Socialist Action:** Group formed by Nat and Sylvia Weinstein, Les Evans, and other Trotskyists in 1983 upon their expulsion from the Socialist Workers Party, which had replaced Trotskyist ideas with those of Fidel Castro. Socialist Action began publishing a militant left newspaper and applied to join the Fourth International (USFI), the largest federation of Trotskyists in the world. Current national secretary of Socialist Action is Jeff Mackler, one of the leaders of The Mobilization to Free Mumia Abu-Jamal. Website found at: http://www.Socialistaction.org/

**Socialist Alternative:** Known as the Labor Militant until they changed their name in 1999. This group was founded in 1986 by supporters of the British Militant Tendency (which had gained much attention for their clandestine entry into the Labor Party in the early 1980's) in the hopes of forming an international network. (They succeeded in forming such a network, which is now known as the Committee for a Workers International CWI.) Socialist Alternative opposes both Black and Irish nationalism. They want an American style of the Labor Party to "fight for the end of domination of big business over U.S. society through nationalization of the commanding heights of the economy." Website found at: http://www.Socialistalternative.org/

**Socialist Labor Party:** Founded in Newark, New Jersey, in 1877 as the Workingmen's Party of America, the party that would become the Socialist Labor Party was a confederation of small Marxist parties from throughout the United States, becoming the first nation-wide Socialist party and only the second one of the so-called "third parties" (the Prohibition Party being the first). In 1976, the SLP ran its last Presidential race, and hasn't run many campaigns since then. They recently have been having trouble even funding their newspaper, _The People_. Due to their die-hard, puritanical politics, the SLP is likely to continue to whither away, much like the Prohibition Party has. Website found at: http://www.slp.org/

**Socialist Party USA:** The Socialist Party USA is one of the heirs to the Socialist Party of Eugene V. Debs and Norman Thomas. Formed as the "Debs Caucus" in the old Socialist Party, the founders of the SP-USA were the most left-wing of the forces who opposed the right-wing leadership which renamed the old Socialist Party as Social Democrats USA (SDUSA). The party has consequently grown from 600 in nearly 1,500 in just the past 5 years. The SP publishes a magazine, _The Socialist_, and an internal discussion bulletin, _ARISE!_ Website found at: http://www.sp-usa.org/

**Socialist Workers Party:** Formed on January 1, 1938, from the Communist League of America after it was expelled from the Socialist Party by the SP's moderate leadership. They came under severe criticism everywhere when they sued the Marxist Internet Archive for posting several Trotsky works that the SWP had copyrighted. This shriveled-up and dying group is a fitting end to the revolutionary party Trotsky dreamed of. Website found at: http://www.themilitant.com/index.shtml

 **Solidarity:** Formed in 1986 from the fusion of the International Socialists, Socialist Unity, and Workers' Power. Solidarity was named after the Polish _Solidarnosc_ — at that time an independent labor union that challenged the Soviet Union from the left. Recently, discussions of "Left Refoundation" have also been initiated between Solidarity and groups such as Left Turn, Freedom Road Socialist Organization, and Detroit's Trotskyist League. Further, many members of the organization are also interested in stronger relations (if not a merger) with the Socialist Party USA. Hopefully, this sort of initiative on Solidarity's part will continue. Besides publishing _Against the Current_, Solidarity also publishes an internal discussion bulletin, _Solidarity News_. Website found at: http://www.solidarity-us.org/

**Spartacist League:** Originally formed as the "Revolutionary Tendency" of the Socialist Workers Party, the Spartacist League was formed in 1964 when they were expelled from the SWP for not supporting the Cuban revolution, as well as opposing the SWP's part in the "revisionist" United Secretariat of the Fourth International (USFI). The Spartacists have been known to become violent at meetings of the ISO and DSA. Two SL front organizations are the Partisan Defense Committee (dedicated to "defending class-war prisoners") and the Prometheus Research Library (a collection of historical Trotskyite documents). Overall, the Spartacist League is one of the most sectarian and ultra-left groups in the American Left.  Website found at: http://www.spartacist.org/

**Workers World Party:** The Workers World Party was founded in 1959 when he left the Socialist Workers Party. Overall, Workers World is one of the most authoritarian groups on the Left today. Website found at: http://www.spartacist.org/

# Appendix B:
# *5 MINUTES TO FREEDOM!*

By Jon Haupt

## A FIVE-MINUTE HANDBOOK FOR GUN-RIGHTS ACTIVISTS
I've been a gun-rights activist for nearly 10 years. I wasted a lot of time for the first five years because no one gave me the rule book you are now reading. Maybe that's because no one had written it. This is the stuff I wish I had known starting on day one. If you've just arrived at this party, the next five minutes you spend reading this might save you five years of otherwise wasted time and energy. If you've been in the gun-rights game for a while, this handbook will be the fastest refresher courseyou've ever taken.

This past year I've received a lot of mail from jittery gun owners who are finally waking up to what's happening to our Right to Keep and Bear Arms (RKBA). This handbook is mostly for them. If the rules I list below scare off a few folks, so be it. I want to tell it like it really is—to give a quick snapshot of the tips, tricks and tactics that actually work in RKBA activism. The bad news is that this is not a complete list of the rules.

The good news is that there will never be a complete list of rules. The rules listed below are based on my own experience from working thousands of hours with down and dirty RKBA activist pros. I am deeply grateful to all of them. They know who they are. Some of these rules have been followed for so long by old-time activists that they have forgotten what the original rules were. It's time to list them again. And sneak in a couple of new ones. So read them and weep, or read them and rejoice.

**NO ONE IS AS INTERESTED AS YOU ARE.** Nowadays everyone's attention span and time are limited. Be grateful if you get anyone's attention on our issue, even for a few seconds. Some wannabe activists come in like a lion, then disappear. Take whatever you get from any volunteer. Praise and thank them. Don't be disappointed when they drift away. They will. But some come back. Keep the light on for them.

**THE NRA STINKS.** So does GOA, SAF, JPFO, and any or all of the rest of the gun-rights groups. At the same time, all of these organizations are the best thing since sliced bread. We won't keep our rights without them. It's normal to love them and hate them at the same time. Be sure your complaints about them go to the person who can do something about your problem. Never give up your membership—it's much easier to fix things from the inside. Avoid griping in public—our opponents love it when we do. Always handle our dirty laundry behind closed doors. Always.

**THERE IS NO MAGIC BULLET.** There is no single answer, rule, or solution. Never has been, and never will be. None of us will write the single brilliant letter to the editor or internet message that will miraculously turn everything around. Keep steadily busy. Do as much as you can, whenever you can. Anything you do counts, but some things count more than others. Find out what counts. Then do it.

**THERE IS NO FINAL VICTORY.** Preserving RKBA is an ongoing PROCESS. We are winning and losing battles during this process, but the war will never be over. Becoming active to keep your gun rights is a lot like cleaning your house: it's thankless and boring work, but necessary. Like dirt, the anti-gun crowd will just keep coming back. Forever. Your activism will keep us winning more than losing. Our opponents count on wearing us down. They love it when one of us (not you, of course) gets discouraged and drops out. When you fully understand and accept the reality that RKBA is a never-ending struggle, you're automatically in the top five percent of all RKBA defenders. Congratulations.

**RKBA ACTIVISM IS BORING.** It's especially boring when you are doing things that really make a difference. Most of us want drama. We want to be entertained. Phone-bank calling, precinct walking, going to RKBA grassroots seminars—suddenly, even a trip to the dentist for a root canal will start to look better. Sorry, but there is no workaround on this aspect. Freedom is not free. It's a pain in the ass. Get used to it, get over it, and get to work.

**USE THE POWER OF FEAR AND GUILT.** Gun owners are susceptible to these emotions. Awaken sleeping RKBA activists by tapping these powerful emotions. Fear and guilt will move mountains— and fill the collection plate, and recruit new members. If gun owners won't become active for themselves, ask them to do it for their families. For their children. For their country. And—this tactic works!—ask them to do it for YOU.

**WATCH OUT FOR MISDIRECTED, TIMEWASTING EFFORTS.** Single emails to elected people is pretty much worthless—unless the official already personally knows you. Internet polls are useless. Online polls make some folks think they are actually doing something. They are not. It's a false sense of accomplishment. It's like bringing a doctor to a dead man. Focus on the stuff that works. If you're going to hunt ducks, go where the ducks are. Coordinated one-issue emails and calls by the hundreds, politicians' staffs *do* notice that.

**POLITICIANS ONLY CARE ABOUT VOTES AND MONEY.** In-person visits, phone calls, and snail mailed, handwritten or hand-typed letters to elected folks help—because politicians know that if you take this much trouble, you and your family and friends will also vote. Courtesy works too. **HOT TIP:** Make yourself known to politicians for issues *other* than gun rights. Don't present yourself as a single-issue person. Praise and help politicians on *their* pet projects. Then, when a new gun-control law comes up, your opinion will seem especially credible. Otherwise, you will soon be stereotyped and discounted as a single issue voter.

**ANOTHER HOT TIP:** Politicians have to explain why they vote Yes or No on proposed laws. Sometimes they really need your help in composing explanations to their constituents. If you want your elected official to vote No on a seemingly popular new gun-control law, she might be more willing if you give her a "back door"—a good, common-sense explanation that she can give to all of her constituents.

**GET THE RIGHT PEOPLE IN OFFICE IN THE FIRST PLACE.** If we have the right people in power, antigun laws will not be passed. Period. The laws are what matter. This concept is so simple many folks can't see it, just like they can't "see" the air they breathe. The anti-rights crowd can hold all the gun-control seminars and news conferences they want, but nothing will happen unless they can pass more laws. This fact tells you about the how, what, where, when, why, and with whom you should be spending your time, energy, and money. Politicians pass laws. Therefore, you must get involved in politics to protect your gun rights. There is just no way to get around this. Sorry. I don't like politics either. Bummer!

**STOP THE SABER RATTLING—NOW!** Avoid those shrill folks who sound threatening or talk about doomsday. It's a waste of your time. These noisy folks remind me of a couple in a failing marriage who only talk about a getting a divorce instead of talking about their real problems. If they don't solve their problems, separation or divorce becomes the inevitable outcome. Some people get pumped up on silly fantasy scenarios. I do not.

**ARM YOURSELF WITH ACCURATE INFORMATION.** Paradoxically, bad information or misinformation is a plague in the so-called Information Age. When you write or talk about firearms issues, use only the facts, the truth, and the provable. Verify any quotes that you use. Back up your generalizations with powerful and specific examples. Get on the Internet, and get your likeminded friends online. Join several of the hundreds of net communities that will keep you informed instantly and completely about our special issues. Information is power!

**IGNORE MEDIA SPIN AND THE NEWS WAVES.** It's far too easy to go bonkers reacting to the latest media-driven crisis. Don't let the media push your buttons. The RKBA grassroots pros I know do not overreact to crises. In fact, most of the ultra-pros that I know do not react at all to media hysteria. Bashing the media about their bias is not productive. Some gun owners use media bias as an excuse to do nothing—because the situation seems so overwhelming and hopeless. Truth is, if you are a busy activist—already steadily doing stuff that matters—you will find the media reacting to *you*. Be friendly and polite with them—not hostile. Become a reliable source of information for them. And just keep on being *active*.

**JUST SHOW UP.** It's been said that 80 percent of success is showing up. Being there. Showing up to vote. Showing up at an RKBA seminar. At your assemblyman's office. At a city-council meeting. My father's favorite motto: "Your actions speak so loud that I can't hear a word you're saying." Your "silent" activism can be a model for others. What will your three hunting buddies think when they find out you spent an afternoon handing out brochures door-to-door for a pro-gun politician?

**DON'T MESS WITH TRUE BELIEVERS.** In the time you spend trying to convert one hard-core antigun person to our side, you could have gone out and motivated and organized 20 people who already think like you do. Go with the flow. It's easier on your nerves, and much more effective. Personally, I have converted several anti-rights true believers, but never again! Lots of NRA members are not registered voters. A lot of gun owners aren't NRA members. Even more folks have no idea of their elected officials' positions on gun issues. Where is your time most effectively spent? Think about this before spending an hour writing a clever response to a silly message you found on the Internet.

**SIMPLICITY STILL MATTERS.** The old rule, Keep It Super Simple (KISS), is as important as it ever was. It applies to web postings, planning, speeches—everything. And keep it short. And keep it sweet: don't ever ridicule or insult anyone. Did you notice that I did *not* say, "Keep It Simple, *Stupid*?"

**YOU ARE ALL ALONE.** Well, not quite alone. You do have some help. The NRA has a staff of several hundred. There is no way humanly possible that "the NRA" can put out all the brush fires started by the anti-rights crowd. Pro-gun national groups give direction and information—but they cannot save your rights. Only *you* can save *your* rights. You are 100 percent responsible. When you fully accept this reality, you are automatically in the top one percent of all RKBA activists.

**THE HIDDEN BONUS OF GUN RIGHTS ACTIVISM.** The more involved you get with firearms freedom, the more you will realize that your single issue actually complements and protects other human-rights issues. Personally, I am deeply offended by many aspects of today's culture. When I focus my activism on RKBA, I can often sense I am making a measurable difference. All rights—like all humans—are connected.

**WHEN IN DOUBT, JUST DO SOMETHING.** Sometimes we don't know what will work. Sometimes the rule is that there are no rules. I once wrote an essay I thought was mediocre at best. Five years later, I'm still receiving mail about it. Don't hesitate to try something new and innovative—get it out on the table! Often your finest essay or brilliant letter will not be acknowledged, or you will just get a form letter response. But that letter to the editor that you dashed off in a few minutes appears in tomorrow's newspaper! Go figure. Better yet, try not to figure. Trust yourself, trust your instincts—and just do something.

I'll see you in the trenches.

## Appendix C:
## *VOTER CONTACT FORM*

☐ Name:
☐ Email Address:
☐ Phone Number:
☐ Hot Button Issue:

Confirmation on:
    ☐ Voter Registration Completed and MAILED
    ☐ Confirm Email
    ☐ Confirm Phone
    ☐ Hot Button Issue

Interim Re-contact
    Date
    Date
    Date
    Date

Get them to the polls...BE SURE THEY INTEND TO VOTE

☐ BE SURE THEY KNOW WHERE THEIR POLLING PLACE IS LOCATED
    Polling location for this voter:

☐ OFFER TO DRIVE THEM TO THE POLLING PLACE IF NECESSARY

# Appendix D:
## *THE LIBERTY POLL*

© Copyright by Attorney Michael P. Anthony, Author Alan Korwin and Syndicated Columnist Vin Suprynowicz

### "Hello candidate -- what's the purpose of government?"

It's time to start asking tough questions the "news" media avoids, to really find out what sort of leaders we are about to elect.

Although reporters can make you think they play hardball with candidates, truly fundamental questions are rarely part of the mix. The Liberty Poll makes this dramatically clear -- it is a fresh approach designed to examine candidates' knowledge and views of:

1 - Our constitutional form of government and their role in it,
2 - The separate powers of federal and state government, and
3 - Constitutionally guaranteed civil and human rights.

Politicians have tended to express shock, or to simply stammer when asked about such things. Some suddenly find they're late for a meeting, and hurriedly duck out. They will take an oath to preserve, protect and defend the Constitution if they are elected to public office. Do they know what that means? Find out by making them take The Liberty Poll. Reporters could win awards if they injected these revealing questions into the national forum.

You should tell your local news media about The Liberty Poll. Next time you see a "newsmaker" yourself, instead of asking about corruption or progress on project X, try asking some of these questions instead, and see what happens.

In these days of expensive sound bites and slogan campaigning, this is an eye-popping opportunity for voters to see their future representatives' views on the offices they seek, and to avoid the wedge issues and glossy funding promises that politicos like because they find them safe (and well rehearsed).

The short and sweet questions below are followed by detailed, in-depth queries from the three co-authors of The Liberty Poll. Ask yourself, "Why don't news people ever ask questions like this?"

## POLICY QUESTIONS

1 - If you are elected to the office you seek:

a) what laws will you repeal;
b) what taxes will you reduce or eliminate;
c) what government agencies will you shrink or close?

2 - Would you support criminal penalties:

a) for politicians who violate their oath of office;
b) for bureaucrats who act outside the powers delegated to them?

3 - When did you last read the state and federal Constitutions?

4 - Should someone who has sworn an oath to preserve, protect and defend the Constitution, but who then votes to allocate tax funds to programs or departments not authorized by that Constitution, be removed from office?

5 - Can you name any current areas of government operations that are outside the authority delegated to government?

6 - Can you name areas where government might serve the public interest, but where it has no authority to act? If not, is it still accurate to say we have "government of limited powers"? Does this matter?

7 - As a candidate for a state or federal office, can you think of any ways to improve enforcement of the 10th Amendment (the states

and the people retain powers not delegated to the federal government)?

## ISSUE QUESTIONS

8 - With regard to jury trials, should judges be required to inform jurors that they have the power, in the sanctity of the jury room, to decide whether a law in question is just, or constitutional? Should schools teach this?

9 - With regard to due process, should judges be allowed to prevent defendants from presenting a defense on constitutional grounds if they so choose?

10 - With regard to the war on drugs, is the war succeeding? When could it be declared a success, the expense of waging it cease, and the tax-based infrastructure surrounding it be decreased or dismantled? If it can't be declared a success, when might it be declared a failure and brought to a close? How do you respond to critics who say the war on some drugs is really just a federal-agent jobs program that provides price supports for the cartels?

11 - With regard to law enforcement, are you in favor of police being allowed to use deadly force when absolutely necessary to protect innocent lives from criminal attack? Do you believe that people, even people with no training of any kind, have less right to defend themselves than the authorities do?

12 - With regard to the right to keep and bear arms, would you support gun laws that would specifically disarm religious individuals, either on the way to or at religious services? Would this be OK as long as all religions were treated equally?

13 - With regard to establishing a federal ID number for every American, would you vote to enable or block such legislation if it were proposed? Which part of the Constitution would authorize such controls over citizens?

14 - With regard to asset-forfeiture laws and policies, describe how these are permissible under the Constitution. If elected, would you do anything to change current asset-forfeiture law?

15 - If elected to the office you seek, would you support legislation to license writers or register printing presses? Would you support legislation to license publishers to help control "hate speech?" Why would an honest writer or publisher object to such a program? If you cannot justify licensing writers, on what basis could you justify licensing gun owners?

The Liberty Poll was developed by attorney Michael P. Anthony, author Alan Korwin and syndicated columnist Vin Suprynowicz and is used by permission. Thanks.

# References:

[1] _"There Is Only The Fight...": An Analysis of the Alinsky Model_, Hillary Diane Rodham (Clinton), Graduate Thesis, Honors Program, Wellesley College, Wellesley, Mass., May 2, 1969

[2] _The Wall Street Journal_, Peggy Noonan former Reagan speechwriter, decried the continued suppression of "the Rosetta Stone of Hillary studies." Copyright © 2005

[3] _The Intelligent Woman's Guide to Socialism and Capitalism_, George Bernard Shaw, Copyright © 1928, Brentano's Publishers

[4] _Rules for Radicals, A Pragmatic Primer for Realistic Radicals_, Saul David Alinsky, Copyright © 1971, ISBN: 0-394-71738-8, , (My copy: Vintage Books Edition, softbound, March 1972)

[5] _The Agitator_, Ryan Lizza, Copyright © 2007, (from _The New Republic_, March 19, 2007)

[6] _Liberal Fascism_, Jonah Goldberg, Copyright © 2007, ISBN: 978-0-385-51184, Doubleday

[7] _Students for a Democratic Society (SDS) The Port Huron Statement (1962)_, various SDS authors, Copyright © 1962, ISBN: 0-88286-173-5, (My copy: Charles H. Kerr Publishing Co., Sixties Series, Copyright © 1990,)

[8] _Reveille for Radicals_, Saul David Alinsky, Copyright © 1946, ISBN-13: 978-0679721123 (Vintage Books),

[9]   *Objectivist Ethics*, Paper delivered by Ayn Rand at the
      University of Wisconsin Symposium on "Ethics in Our Time,"
      Madison Wisconsin, February 9, 1961, Copyright © 1961 by
      Ayn Rand, reprinted in *The Virtue of Selfishness*, ISBN: 0-
      451-16393-1, (SIGNET Edition, published by The New
      American Library, Division of Penguin Putnam, Inc.)

[10]  *The Liberal Mind, The Psychological Causes of Political
      Madness*, Lyle H. Rossiter, Jr. M.D., Copyright © 2006, ISBN-
      13: 978-0977956302, , Publisher: Free World Books, LLC
      (October 30, 2006)

[11]  *U.S. Constitution*, various authors, Copyright ©1776

[12]  *ECODEFENSE: A Field Guide to Monkeywrenching*, Dave
      Foreman, Copyright © 1985, ISBN 0-933285-01-9, (Earth
      First! Books)

[13]  *Guerrilla Warfare*, Che Guevara, Original Copyright ©1961,
      Copyright © 1985 by University of Nebraska Press, ISBN 0-
      8032-7010-0

## About the Author...

*Charly Gullett was originally trained as a photo-journalist in the U.S. Army Defense Information School.  However, he spent most of his adult life as a self-taught applications engineer specializing in Robotics, Digital Instrumentation and Analog Computer Design. Retiring in 1996 from Intel Corp. as a senior technical author, Gullett was awarded their highest individual achievement award for his ground-breaking work in Artificial Intelligence.  Additionally, Gullett's career has included work as a professional photographer, cabinet maker, college teacher, a firearms dealer, and a professional artist who has illustrated over thirty books as well as authoring two books on action shooting and gunsmithing antique firearms.*

**WARFIELD PRESS**

PRESCOTT, ARIZONA

6976309R0

Made in the USA
Lexington, KY
08 October 2010